IDAHO'S PLACE IN THE SUN

by
Helen M. Newell

Helen M. Newell

SYMS-YORK
BOISE, IDAHO

Manuscript of this book was read for accuracy of detail
by Dr. Merle W. Wells, Director, Idaho Historical Society.

Published by
Syms-York Company
Boise, Idaho

Dedicated to the memory of Deborah Davis and Hoyt Cooper, and to all other teachers who have brought history to life for generations of Idaho students.

.

APPRECIATION

The author's grateful thanks to these friends who helped bring about this book:

Rosalie Barbour

Dr. John A. Caylor

Gwendolyn Deal

Sister M. Alfreda Elsensohn

Marney and Duane Garrett

Dorine Goertzen

Utahna Hall

Virginia Hibbs

Grace E. Jordan

Bernice and T. Bailey Lee, Jr.

Lauchlin S. McCurry

Marie Milette (who started it all)

Ardella Morrissey

Helen Peshak Newell

Robert P. Newell

Hilma Peterson

Gail Price

Orville Reddington

John Rogge

Ellis Stoddard

Norma Stout

Jean D. Swanson

Faith Turner

Dr. Merle W. Wells

Marge Williams

And to these organizations:

Appaloosa Horse Club Association

Boise Public Library

Idaho Dept. of Tourism and Industrial Development

Idaho Historical Society

Idaho State Library

Kellogg Chamber of Commerce

Montana Historical Society

University of Idaho Extension Service

U.S. Bureau of Land Management

U.S. Bureau of Reclamation

IDAHO'S PLACE IN THE SUN

Contents

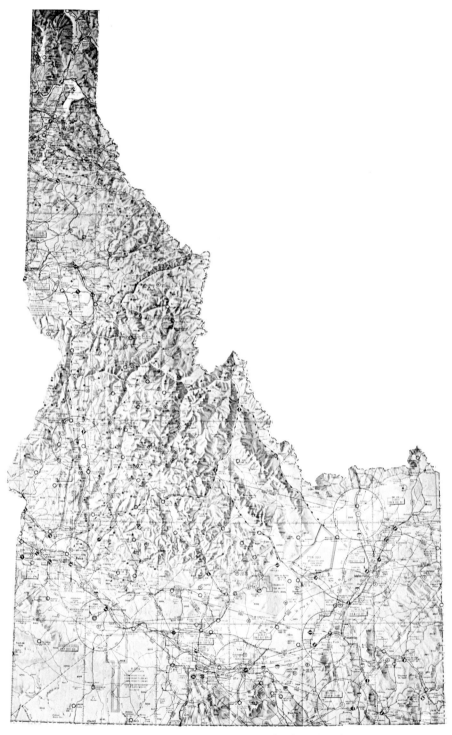

Taken from Idaho Aeronautical Chart

VI

Chapter 1

BEFORE WE WROTE HISTORY

T HE LAND on which Idaho sits has been here for millions —even billions—of years, but unless you are a geologist you will probably be satisfied with a few facts about the last 15,000, when man appeared on the scene.

Men and animals live near water, and it is in the sediments of the Snake River Plain we find our evidence: the butchered bones of animals, and the points of weapons that hunters used. We have found bones of elephants, camels, bison, mountain sheep, and the ground sloth, (that bear with the snout). There also come to light from time to time on farms and in excavations, bones of animals that preceded man and became extinct before he arrived: mastodon (our family had a mastodon tooth as big as my head, out of the excavation for the American Falls powerhouse), mammoth, giant ox, and a horse that geologists have given the impressive geographical name of Plesippus shoshonensis. Archaeologists have retrieved many bones from the Hagerman Valley sandstone, a good preservative cover. Most of these are now in the Smithsonian Institution in Washington, D. C.

Our state's surface was formed by successions of violent happenings: drownings of the land by invading seas; volcanic eruptions and underground upheavals; glaciers that dammed rivers into vast lakes; and weathering.

A shallow ocean rolled in over the land and in the course of time it deposited in eastern Idaho, sediments 8,000 feet deep. These sediments contained seashells which today form our phospate deposits near Pocatello, used in fertilizer and detergents.

Upheavals from pressures inside the earth elevated our mountains. They were then shaped by spring floods that cut gullies and canyons, and by rampaging weather—rain, snow and wind.

Erupting volcanoes brought minerals and volcanic ash to the upper soil, making it wonderfully fertile whenever water could reach it. They also brought gold, silver, lead and zinc to a level where miners were able to discover them. The boiling heat in the earth left hot water springs all over the state. Have you waded in the Payette River near Grandjean and felt the water ice cold around your ankles and hot on the bottom of your feet? Volcanic activities left even stranger things, like the fantastic black landscapes of the Craters

Lava flow, Craters of the Moon National Monument, near Arco, Idaho.
Courtesy Idaho Dept. of Tourism and Industrial Development

of the Moon, where you can imagine you are an astronaut just descending from your rocket. They blew out hollows underground, such as the Shoshone Ice Caves, the most famous of Idaho caves, located about 18 miles north of the city of Shoshone, just off U.S. Highway 93. They spread the mysterious lavas in eastern Idaho where rivers sink out of sight, and reappear in the form of the Thousand Springs in Hagerman Valley 150 miles away. And in that valley there are places you can put your ear to the ground and hear vast rumblings like an ocean rolling.

Idaho is full of amazing things.

Chapter 2

IDAHO'S APPALOOSA

URGED BY THE Sixth Grade of Eagle elementary school, the 1975 Idaho Legislature named the Appaloosa our official State Animal.

The Appaloosa has been important in our area since the beginning of our history. It arrived here more than 100 years before the white man did. It came a very long way, thousands of miles from Tibet, thousands of years through history. We first know of it as the horse of the Mongols. Later, the Persians got hold of these horses, and wrote poems about them. The Chinese made porcelain statues of them. They came to America by way of Spain, coming across the ocean with the conquistadors to conquer Mexico.

There were not many of the horses in the New World at first, but they were a strong breed and they multiplied and survived. They are a famous example of the truth that a good thing endures. Moving northward by trade and theft, by 1730 they had reached our Snake River Plateau and the Shoshoni Indians. When the Shoshonis traded them to the Nez Perce Indians, the horses had arrived at their natural home.

The Nez Perce seemed to have an inborn knowledge of how to strengthen the breed's best qualities. Lewis and Clark wrote in their Journals that the Nez Perce were more skilled in this science than even the horse lovers of Virginia.

Horses made a great change in the life of the tribe. They could ride across the mountains to Montana for buffalo hunts. They could travel long distances to battle other tribes for supremacy. In a century they had developed a breed that was fast and tireless, well suited to the climate and country of north Idaho. The Nez Perce raised great herds of thousands of Appaloosa. It was because of these splendid horses that Chief Joseph and his people in 1877 were able to outsmart the best of the U.S. Army for six months and 1300 miles.

When the Nez Perce were finally overtaken and forced onto a reservation, the Army gathered up their spotted horses to sell and the breed was scattered and lost until the 1930s, although spotted colts popped up in remudas all over the cattle country. Circuses hunted for them to train for trick riding. Whenever stockmen got hold of one, they held onto it to increase the breed. Nowadays there are

Governor Cecil D. Andrus signing bill naming the Appaloosa horse Idaho's official state animal.

Photo by Kenneth C. Poertner

many organizations and magazines devoted to the increase and improvement of the Appaloosa. There are about 10,000 of the breed in Idaho today.

The spotted horses have been called by many names through history. Their Idaho name came from a small river in the Nez Perce country called by French fur traders the "Palouse"—"the river with the green meadows." Near the mouth of this river was one of the leading breeders of the spotted horses, and settlers came to refer to them as the "Palouse horses." In use, the word gradually developed into "Appaloosa."

People who don't know a lot about horses often suppose an Appaloosa is just some kind of a pinto or "paint." But a pinto's markings, usually large patches of dark spread over a white background, are simply an accident of a combination of parents. The markings of the Appaloosa, on the other hand, came down with it through all its long history.

Sometimes these markings are like a leopard's, small dark spots all over a light body. Sometimes the front half of the horse is a solid color, and there are spots only over the rear half. Under its coat the Appaloosa's skin is dark. Its nostrils, lips and under-belly are mottled pink. Its hoofs, which are unusually hard and bear up well in rough and rocky country, are striped white and black. A particular characteristic of the breed is a thin mane and tail. Sometimes the hair on the tail is so thin, it looks almost like a rat tail. The Appaloosa's eyes look very wide-awake because they are circled with white, as people's eyes are. Most horses' eyes are completely dark.

When you are in Helena, Montana, be sure to go to the State Capitol building and see the great painting of an Appaloosa horse by Charles Russell.

Charga Belle, grand champion Appaloosa mare, 1973.
Courtesy Appaloosa Horse Association

Lewis and Clark explore the great Northwest.
Print of painting by Dean Cornwell
Courtesy Idaho Historical Society

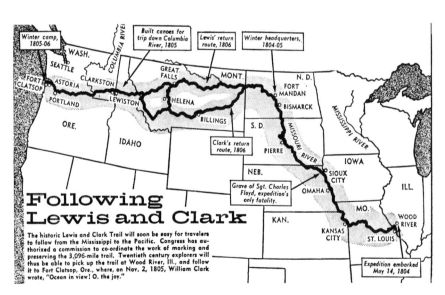

Courtesy Dr. John W. Caylor

Chapter 3

LEWIS AND CLARK

WHEN NAPOLEON Bonaparte ran short of money for his project of conquering the world, he sold the province of Louisiana to the United States. It was not the size Louisiana is today. It stretched all the way from the Mississippi River to the Rocky Mountains, and from the edge of Texas to Canada. It was ½-billion acres of the richest farmland in the world, and it cost the United States about three cents an acre.

President Thomas Jefferson, a man of large ideas and unusual imagination, was inspired by this purchase. It nearly doubled the size of the United States. How splendid it would be if we could extend it even farther, clear to the Pacific Ocean!

Beyond the Rocky Mountains (in those days sometimes called the "Stony Mountains"), the land didn't belong to anybody—yet. But very soon some country would go after it. A country could get land by winning a war, or by buying it from some other country, or by beating other countries to it in doing three things: first, Discovery; second, Exploration; and third, Settlement.

The United States already had a claim to the Northwest by right of Discovery. Captain Robert Grey, sailing along the Pacific Coast buying furs from the Indians in 1792, discovered the Columbia River pouring out into the ocean. This gave us a claim to all the land from which the water in the Columbia River flowed.

The next step must be Exploration. South of Canada, no white man had crossed the land that extended between the Rocky Mountains and the Pacific Ocean. President Jefferson thought it was just the right moment for us to get ahead of Russia who was busy fur-trading along the Alaska coast, Spain who was doing the same in her California colonies, and Great Britain with her fur-trading stations in Canada.

The President had a high regard for his private secretary, Captain Meriwether Lewis. Jefferson appointed him, and Lewis's comrade of Indian wars, Captain William Clark, to lead an exploring party through this country. They would take boats and follow all the way up the Missouri River, which began on the east side of the Rocky Mountains. Beyond the mountains was the unexplored. But they knew that over the Continental Divide, streams would flow down the west side of the Rockies and join together to become the Columbia

River, which would flow into the Pacific Ocean as Captain Grey had discovered.

The party loaded one keel-boat and two dugout canoes and on May 14, 1804, shoved them into the lowest part of the Missouri River, near St. Louis, and began working their way north against the current. Winter halted them after six months, and they set up camp where Bismarck, North Dakota is now, and spent the winter among the Mandan Indians.

Here we meet Sacajawea, who is almost as famous as Lewis and Clark. Sacajawea was a Shoshoni Indian girl, born in an Idaho valley. When she was about twelve, she went with her family on a buffalo hunt over the mountains into Montana lands, and was taken captive by an enemy tribe. She lived with them as a slave until Charbonneau, a French-Canadian, bought and married her.

The expedition hired Charbonneau to go along as an interpreter with any Indians they should meet; and Sacajawea, hoping for a chance to see her own people, went along, carrying her new baby son on her back. She turned out to be very valuable for the safety of the party. Indians, seeing a woman with a papoose, knew at once that this wasn't a war party, and held their arrows until after investigation.

In April, 1805, the party started west, with a Mandan guide to help them through the Rockies and find the Shoshonis. The Shoshonis were great people for horses, and the expedition would need horses to get themselves and their supplies across the mountains when they could no longer travel by boat.

The Great Falls of the Missouri River were an immense barrier in their route. Before dams were built on that river, Great Falls was *really* great, boats couldn't get through at all. The party had to portage for miles around them. They cut round sections from the trunks of cottonwood trees to make little wheels for carts to haul the heavy dugout canoes, and a long line of men dragged them by ropes over the rough ground. It took a whole month to get past the Falls.

Five different men kept journals of the trip. They wrote about everything that happened every day, and described trees and plants and flowers and birds and animals, and kept a record of the weather. Captain Clark was the map maker. He also drew pictures of animals and birds and plants, and Indians they met. Captain Clark was a very intelligent and skilled man, but he hadn't had much schooling, and his spelling will amaze you if you ever look at his journal in the library.

Another entertaining thing about Captain Clark was his marvelous negro servant, York. The Mandan Indians were astonished at him, for they had never seen a black man before. They rubbed his arm with a wet finger to see if the paint would come off! This tickled York, who had a great sense of fun, and he invented all kinds of tall yarns about himself to entertain them. Later on, in Idaho, the Nez Perce Indians were just as astonished by the rest of the expedition, for *they* had never seen a white man. They thought everybody should be red-skinned.

The expedition brought along knives, red cloth and beads as gifts for the Indians, or to trade for food. There was a special "Peace Medal" to present to important chiefs. Very few medals survive today, but the Idaho Historical Society is the proud possessor of one. You can see it, a battered silver medallion about 3½ inches in diameter, hanging in a glass case on the reception desk of the State Historical Museum. On one side is a picture of President Jefferson, and on the other, two hands clasped in friendship. It is dated 1801.

After a rugged trip into the eastern slopes of the Rocky Mountains, by good fortune the party found an Indian trail that led them through the pass that today we call Lemhi Pass, ten miles east of the present settlement of Tendoy.

Sacajawea grew excited as she began to recognize landmarks. Nearing what is now the Montana-Idaho line, they met a group of Indians on the trail. A young Indian woman stepped forward, and Sacajawea rushed to meet her as she recognized a childhood playmate who had been captured with herself, but had later escaped. But her greatest joy came when she recognized the chief of this Shoshoni tribe as her brother, Cameahwait! A monument honors Sacajawea's approximate birthplace a few miles north of old Fort Lemhi on State Highway 28.

Lewis and Clark had hoped to build new canoes and travel down the first big stream on the west side of the Continental Divide, headed for the Pacific Ocean. Exploration now convinced them the Salmon River was not navigable by canoe. They bought forty horses from the Indians, and with a Shoshoni guide, rode north along the North Fork of the Salmon River, crossing the Bitterroot Mountains into what is now Montana. At a point near present Missoula, they found the Indian trail we now call the Lolo. This led them through a pass (now called the Lolo Pass) through the Bitterroots into Idaho again.

Finding food enough for thirty people was a problem on the whole trip, but in the Idaho country it was scarcest of all. The scenery was beautiful, but Idaho was never a land of plenty. Even the natives lived in a nearly starving condition much of the year. In summer the salmon came up the rivers from the ocean to spawn. There was some game, deer and elk and moose, and now that the Indians had horses they could ride over into the Montana buffalo country and bring back meat for winter. There were huckleberries and service berries most summers, and the camas lily and other bulbs were dug up to be dried and ground into meal to make bread. But generally there was too great a scarcity of food to allow any extra to trade. When the explorers had nothing else to eat, they killed some of their colts for food.

By the end of September they reached the banks of the Clearwater River, about forty miles from where Lewiston now is. (Lewiston is named for Captain Lewis, and across the bridge in Washington is Clarkston, named for Captain Clark.) Here at last was a stream that could start them on the last leg of their journey to the Pacific Ocean. They made camp and settled down to build five big canoes. The camp was called "Ahsahka," which means "Canoe Camp." At Ahsahka today you can see a dugout canoe made by a Nez Perce Indian, which is exactly like the canoes the Lewis and Clark expedition made.

This is almost the end of the story. The Clearwater River carried them down to the Snake River, the Snake carried them to the Columbia River, and on November 15, 1805, they reached the Pacific Ocean at a point near where Astoria is now located. They had traveled 4,000 miles. They had stolen a march on Great Britain and Russia and Spain in exploring the lands drained by the Columbia River.

Lewis and Clark and their party are our earliest heroes (and heroine!) in Idaho. They had the same high spirit of adventure and bravery, heading into the unknown, as our astronauts today, heading for the moon.

They labored their boats against the current of the Missouri River for 2500 miles. They sweltered up steep mountain-sides in summer, their feet and hands and faces froze in winter. They were dumped from boats into icy waters. There was hardly ever enough to eat, and they were often parched with thirst. Their small party stood up to the menacing Sioux Indians. They were charged by buffalo, they battled grizzly bears. Clouds of mosquitoes sucked their blood and prickly pear cactus cut through their moccasins.

And through the endurance of these dangers and miseries, this little band completed the second requirement of the United States for a claim to the Northwest: the requirement of Exploration.

Chapter 4

BEAVER BONANZA

I N THE BEGINNING the only thing Idaho had that white men wanted, was furs. There was a tremendous market for them, both in Europe and in China, and their value as a prestige symbol was so great that there were laws about who could wear them. Only the aristocracy could wear the fine furs. Ordinary folk could wear sheepskin or rabbit fur if they could afford them. And the most prestigious of symbols for a man was the tall handsome beaver hat.

A few years after Lewis and Clark struggled their toilsome way across the Idaho mountains, the trappers came. For the next thirty years, thousands of men trapped the banks of rivers, lakes and every likely stream. Millions of dollars worth of furs went east to the fur auctions; and the beaver and muskrat and mink and otter were very nearly wiped out in this country.

The first great fur company was the Hudson's Bay company, a group of wealthy Englishmen chartered in 1670 with a monopoly of the fur trade "on all lands watered by streams flowing into Hudson's Bay." On a map of Canada in your atlas you can see what an immense area this included.

After the English defeated the French, and Canada was ceded to England in 1763, many individual English fur traders began to work in Canada on their own. In the interests of holding their own against Hudson's Bay, they finally combined into a company of their own, the North West Fur Company. This company's intention was to work the territory south and west of the territory of the Hudson's Bay monopoly, although they often trespassed.

David Thompson, a partner in the new company, in 1809 followed the Pend Oreille River south, and built a log trading post on Lake Pend Oreille near the present town of Hope—first building in Idaho's history. Thompson called it Kullyspell House after nearby Indians that we call Kalispell. The two log buildings were burned some years later in a forest fire and the exact location lost. In 1923 remnants of the old fireplace chimneys were rediscovered, and citizens of Bonner County erected a monument on the site.

Most of the early British traders were remarkable men with various talents. David Thompson was a devoted geographer and map

The Trapper.

Pen and ink sketch by Charles M. Russell
Reproduction courtesy Montana Historical Society

maker. He spent 23 years surveying and mapping the country worked by the North West Company. It seems odd to us today to find these early maps of Idaho in the British Museum in London.

The trappers, whatever their nationality, were very different from other people. Some of them worked for wages for a company, some were "free trappers" who trapped on their own and sold the furs to a company. But however they operated, they were loners. It suited them to spend months in the wilderness, without seeing any other human being. They were tough and tireless. They understood the outdoors and animals, and cared little about anything else. They had to find ways to get along with the Indians (they often married Indian women), but they didn't bother to get along with white men. Their whole purpose in life was to get all the furs they could, no matter how. They didn't stop at murder. They had to be without nerves because their lives were in danger night and day. More than half of them would end in violent death, yet they wouldn't trade their way of life with anyone.

The Americans were bound to try for a piece of this rich pie. The first American company was the Missouri Fur Company out of St. Louis. Expedition leader Andrew Henry first tried the streams at Three Forks, Montana, but the Blackfeet, the fiercest of the tribes, caused them so much trouble that they moved down the mountains and built a group of cabins where St. Anthony now is, and called it Fort Henry. Fort Henry wasn't a good place for game, so they had to live mainly on horse meat, and they didn't come back the next season. But Henry's Lake and Henry's Fork remind us that they were there.

The most ambitious American company was John Jacob Astor's. This German boy, who arrived in New York with nothing but imagination, shrewdness, and a driving ambition, was one of our earliest American success stories. Sizing up his new country, he decided the quickest and biggest money was in furs. At first he packed the furs he bought, on his back. When he died at the age of 85, he had the largest fortune that had been acquired in the United States up to that time—thirty million dollars. "Get ahead, give the least, get the most," was his rule. On every dollar he invested, he made eight and he made five dollars on every beaver skin he sent to England, and $30,000 on every shipload to China.

There was a great fur auction in Canton, from where furs were sold all over the East. What a profitable thing it would be, thought Astor, to have the first trading post on our Pacific Coast, to gather furs from all the coastal streams and ship them directly across the Pacific to China. The ships could then be loaded with tea, silk, cotton and porcelain, and brought back to sell in Boston.

Astor immediately organized the Pacific Fur Company. He would send two expeditions, he decided, one by ship to carry the necessary supplies and trading goods, and one by land to lay out the best overland route and spot good trapping areas inland.

His ship "Tonquin" left New York in September 1810 to sail around Cape Horn at the tip of South America, out to the Sandwich Islands (Hawaii) to set up an agency there, then back to the mouth of the Columbia River. The 6½-month trip was one long feud. Captain Thorn was a belligerent man, very determined about his authority, and there were several company partners on board eager to argue with him about who was boss.

Where the Columbia poured out into the ocean, it was very rough and turbulent. Two small boats and eight men were lost, trying to get soundings of water depth. And when the Tonquin finally did succeed in getting into the estuary, their troubles had only begun. The cantankerous captain wouldn't wait for a decision as to the best site to build their fort. He dumped the cargo on land and took twenty-three men sailing up the coast to start trade with the Indians. Unfortunately for them, the first Indian tribe they approached was as cantankerous as the captain. They immediately took offense at his high-handed treatment, and proceeded to kill all the white men and destroy the ship. Only the Indian interpreter escaped to carry back the grim tale to the rest of the party.

The rest of them went ahead and built a large stone fort, naming it Fort Astoria after the head of their company. For trading along the coast, they built a little schooner on a frame they had brought with them. They were in business. But, also, they were in trouble. Everywhere they went inland, the North West trappers were there before them, busily stirring up the Indians against them.

Meanwhile, the overland expedition was running into more hard luck than you would believe possible. The name of its leader, Wilson Price Hunt, has come down in history almost as a synonym for misfortune and suffering. The party was made up of men of courage and endurance, but not much experience in exploring unknown territory, and every decision they made turned out to be the wrong one. They had intended to follow the successful route of Lewis and Clark, but they ran into some trappers who had been at Fort Henry the year before, and were persuaded to go up the Yellowstone River by way of Fort Henry. Then Wilson Price Hunt let his French-Canadian boatmen talk him into leaving their 77 horses at Fort Henry and taking to the Snake River in canoes. From that moment the expedition seemed to be jinxed. The Snake River falls and rapids were not navigable. By long portages they managed to get around the Idaho Falls and the American Falls, but when they came to the whirlpools below where Milner Dam is now ("The Devil's Scuttle Hole" they named this section of the river), canoes were broken up, supplies were lost, a man was drowned.

They struggled along on foot on the high cliffs above the Snake River, suffering from starvation, thirst and exhaustion. The wonder is that as many of the party finally reached Fort Astoria as did.

After more problems and difficulties of the reunited expeditions, the War of 1812 broke out, and Great Britain sent a ship to take over Fort Astoria and rename it Fort George.

The War of 1812 has always been a little hazy in my mind. I knew that Captain Oliver Perry issued a triumphant dispatch from his ship on Lake Erie, "We have met the enemy and they are ours!" I knew "Old Ironsides" had licked a British ship somewhere. I knew the British burned our capital, and while trying to burn Baltimore as well, inspired a young lawyer named Francis Scott Key to write "The Star-Spangled Banner." But just what started the trouble, I was never really certain. Now I find it was a perfectly definite war caused by perfectly definite disagreements. The British were fighting Napoleon, and we Americans insisted on continuing to sell supplies to the French. The British began boarding our ships and taking over their cargoes and sailors. Before long we were popping away at them on the high seas, and heading north to try to take Canada away from them.

When the War of 1812 was settled, in an unsettled kind of way, England and the United States agreed that both would occupy the Northwest territory for the time being. But from then on, they kept a suspicious eye on one another for underhanded plots that might be in progress to get permanent title to the territory.

Spain and Russia had also had claims by Discovery, but Spain had withdrawn her claim to concentrate on California and her lands in the Southwest, while Russia had withdrawn her claim and retired to her interests in Alaska. Great Britain and the United States were left bristling at one another like two bulldogs.

Such an unlikely gentleman as an educated Bostonian built another American trading post in Idaho. It was a rather accidental happening. Nathaniel Wyeth, who had been traveling around the West a good deal, claimed he could supply the Rocky Mountain Fur Company more cheaply than their regular suppliers, the Sublettes, and he signed a contract to do so. But when he arrived with $3,000 worth of goods at the annual trappers' rendezvous at Green River, the Rocky Mountain Company had already bought its supplies from its regular suppliers, and Wyeth was stuck with his expensive trade goods. He decided to open a post of his own, so between the present cities of Pocatello and Blackfoot, he built Fort Hall.

The two British fur companies, after years of bitter rivalry and trying by every trick to drive each other out of fur territories, had given up their fight in 1821 and merged under the Hudson's Bay name, to fight the upstart American fur companies. Company representatives watched Mr. Wyeth run up a homemade flag of unbleached muslin, red flannel and a few patches of blue, over his Fort Hall trading post, and they went straight off to build Fort Boise, about halfway between Fort Hall and Fort Walla Walla. This area wouldn't support two trading posts, but Hudson's Bay planned to draw the trade away from Fort Hall, by methods known to every merchant, and drive Nathaniel Wyeth out of business.

At Fort Boise, Francis Payette, an old hand at this kind of maneuver, began paying the Indians very high prices for furs, and selling supplies to them at very low prices. In less than two years Wyeth sold his failing business to Hudson's Bay at a loss. Then Francis Payette packed up and moved Fort Boise to a little better location, below where Parma is now.

The area had once been good fur territory, but it was getting pretty well trapped out. What Fort Boise is best remembered for, is a stopping place for weary emigrants. Francis Payette was a wonderful host. He had a herd of cows and a flock of chickens, and hogs and sheep, and a garden, and especially, he had a fine cook. Receiving all this generous hospitality, discouraged travelers took heart once more and went on their way much cheered. Francis Payette had trapped in this country very early, and no other man has left his name on so much Idaho geography. We have a city, Payette, a county, a pair of lakes, a river, a national forest. If you want places named for you, plan to be one of the first arrivals.

Of all the men listed as Idaho fur traders, Captain Benjamin Bonneville is the most fun to read about. He had a happy temperament and enjoyed everything that happened to him. This is a little surprising, because he started life in the reign of terror following France's revolution. The Marquis Lafayette helped the family to escape and set themselves up in the New World. An appointment to West Point started Benjamin out on an army career. At military posts along what was then the frontier, he met Indians, trappers and other men from the Far West and became fascinated with the country. Arranging a three-year leave of absence from the army, he got private financial backing for an exploring and trapping expedition, gathering information on the country and the Indian tribes. Of all expedition leaders, Bonneville seems to have undergone the least hardship, trapped the fewest beaver, and had the most fun. It is hardly fair, then, that he should have come down in our history as probably the best known. That is because he turned his journals and maps over to Washington Irving, that colorful and entertaining writer, who proceeded to write "The Adventures of Captain Bonneville," exciting much interest in our Northwest. There is nothing like a good public relations treatment.

Today it seems likely that Captain Bonneville's expedition had an understanding with our Government to act as a kind of undercover outfit to see what the Hudson's Bay Company was up to. If so, it was humorous, because he kept running into a Britisher named William Stewart who appeared to be just traveling around and going on hunting trips, but who was no doubt an undercover agent for the British government, to see what the Americans were up to. They must have been much the same kind of jolly fellows, entertaining each other with their adventurous tales of hunting and trapping.

Captain Bonneville had a special talent for getting along with people, his own men and the Indians. The thick-haired Indians were fascinated by his high, prematurely bald head. With their usual habit of nicknaming everybody, they called him "The Bald Chief," and gathered around whenever he took his hat off. However, all the pictures I have seen of him show a head of black hair, so he must have worn a wig whenever he had his picture taken.

Along about this time, John Jacob Astor visited London and was grieved to discover that fashion was indeed fickle. Beaver hats were going out of style, high silk hats were now the thing. Fur trading would continue for some years, but the high prices were a thing of the past. The beaver bonanza was about over.

Chapter 5

MARIE DORION

U SUALLY INCLUDED as a footnote of Idaho's fur-trapping history is the experience of one woman so extraordinary, it should be told by itself.

With the Wilson Price Hunt party on its overland trip to Astoria, was an interpreter, Pierre Dorion, half-French and half-Indian. His wife, Marie, one of the Iowa Indian tribe, and their two little boys, Baptiste and Paul, came along. On that terrible trip Marie gave birth to a third child, but the baby didn't live.

The Hunt party had been impressed by the trapping possibilities of the valley of the Boise River, and in 1813 they fitted out a small party under the leadership of John Reed, to return and trap in the area. Included with this party was the Dorion family.

The party built a main building where the Boise River runs into the Snake River, on the border between Idaho and Oregon, and then some temporary little huts along their traplines, extending to where Caldwell now is. (On the early maps, the Boise River is called the Reed River, after John Reed.)

Trapping proved very successful. Marie Dorion and her children stayed at the main house, where she dressed furs, cooked, fished and gathered wood. The trappers worked up along the river and slept sometimes in the huts, sometimes in the main house.

On the evening of January 10, 1814, a friendly Indian came riding hard to warn that a war-like band of Snake Indians were in the neighborhood. Marie and her children were alone. She caught a horse, and with her children, hurried up the river to warn the trappers. It was snowing and dark and she lost her way. She made camp as best she could in some protective brush, wrapping the children in a buffalo robe, and waited out the storm. It snowed bitterly all the next day, but on the second day it stopped, and she got her bearings and started on. Right away she saw smoke, and hid the family again. It was the third day before she reached one of the huts. As she approached, one of the trappers, LeClerc, staggered out, mortally wounded. The Indians had come to rob them of their furs, and had killed all the others, including Pierre Dorion.

With great difficulty, Marie got the injured man up on the horse with the children and started to lead the horse back the way she had come. LeClerc was so weak from loss of blood that he soon fell off. Marie made a camp in the snow and tried to do what she could for the poor man, but in the night he died. She covered the body with snow and brush and started again.

When she came near the main house, she took to the woods and considered what she must do. There was no sign of life around the building, all seemed deserted. There had been a good supply of fish on hand at the time she left, and it was now several days since they had eaten. When it was growing dusk, she left the children wrapped in the buffalo robe, and the horse tied in a thicket, and climbed to a high piece of ground where she could get a good look at the house. There was still not any sign of life, it was silent as a tomb.

A tomb is what it was. When she had gathered her courage together to go into the house, a scene of savage butchery met her eyes in the dim light. The trappers there had been scalped and hacked to pieces. Forcing herself to speak, she called the name of each trapper, over and over. There was no answer, no movement. Then, outside the door she glimpsed wolves hunting around, and she hurried back to drive off three or four that were nearing the place where the children were hidden. She gathered wood and built a fire to keep the wolves off, and warmed the children, who were almost frozen. Then she rolled them up again, close to the fire, and forced herself to return to the ghastly house to get food.

There were plenty of fish. She took all she could carry on her back and returned to the children. Building up the fire again, she prepared food and they ate ravenously. The thing they must do, Marie decided, was strike out for the Blue Mountains and try to find the friendly Walla Walla Indians. The snow was deep and the weather was cold. They must take all the food they could carry on the horse. She must go back to the death house once more and bring another load of fish.

She did this, but it took all her strength of mind, and when she returned to the children, she collapsed, and for several days she hardly moved.

Finally she roused herself, packed and loaded the horse, and started over the hills through the trackless snow. They traveled nine days before the horse gave out completely.

Marie found a spot near a mountain spring, protected by an overhanging cliff. She built a little hut of pine branches, grass and moss, and packed snow around it like an igloo. She killed the brave horse that had brought them so far, cut the meat into little strips, and smoke-dried it. The horse hide added a little more cover for the shelter. And there the little family existed for the next fifty-three winter days and nights.

When their food was nearly gone, Marie knew they must move on while they still had the strength. She packed the little bit of meat that was left, and all the covers she could carry on her back, along with the youngest boy, Paul, and taking Baptiste by the hand, she started breaking trail up and across the ridge of mountains.

One would hardly expect the situation could become worse. But the bright sunshine blazed off the snow-covered mountainside all day long into Marie's eyes, and she became snow-blind. There was nothing to do but stop for several days until she could see to go on. At last, fifteen days after leaving their little igloo-hut, they came down onto the plains that would finally bring them to the Walla Walla River. A good distance ahead, Marie thought she could see a column of smoke.

But the last bit of meat was gone. She was too weak to carry Paul any longer. Baptiste was exhausted. Once more wrapping up the children and hiding them in the snow, she marked the place with what brush she could drag up, and then set off with her last strength, barely able to move along. By going a little way, and resting, and going another little way, and resting, through the long night, by morning she had come much closer to the column of smoke. A few steps, and rest, another few steps, and rest.

By noon she reached the Indian camp. It turned out to be the first piece of good fortune in more than two months—it was the Walla Walla tribe she had met two years before, when they rescued the starving Wilson Price Hunt party. They clustered around her with cries of welcome, and hurried back along her dragging footprints to bring the children.

How thankful we are she made it through! Even after 160 years, I think we could scarcely bear it if the grim and valiant struggle of that indomitable woman had come to nothing.

Except for Sacajawea, Marie Dorion is the first woman to step out of Idaho history. An incredible heroine! Stricken with grief and horror and fear, she held onto her sanity and sense, to carry through what she had to do alone. How wonderful is the fortitude of the human spirit. The women of Idaho are awed and proud.

Chapter 6

LAPWAI MISSION

T HE INDIANS learned about the white man's Bible and religion from the explorers. The Nez Perce Indians believed this must be the heart of white people's power, and they wanted to know more about it. They sent four of their men to St. Louis for information and to ask that missionaries be sent to them. Five years passed before the mission board of the Congregational and Presbyterian churches, at Boston, sent their first missionaries across the Rocky Mountains. In 1836 Dr. Marcus Whitman started a mission near Walla Walla for the Cayuse Indians, and Reverend Henry Spalding started one at Lapwai (12 miles above where Lewiston is located) for the Nez Perce.

Coming across the plains, Mr. Spalding noticed the buffalo herds were being killed off in such numbers that they would eventually be wiped out. This would be fatal for the Nez Perce, because the pattern of their life was built around the salmon and the buffalo. Every year they traveled east on the Lolo Trail across the mountains to the plains where the herds lived. They would kill enough buffalo to make dried meat to last them a year, and they cured the hides to make walls, beds and rugs for their tepees. To survive without buffalo, Mr. Spalding thought, the Indians would have to settle on the land and learn to farm. He would teach them.

Mr. Spalding was a remarkably handy man. He knew something about nearly everything. First, they must get a crop planted. He made some wooden plows, but the horses that had pulled his wagon on the long hard trip across the continent, were too worn out to pull the plows. Mr. Spalding journeyed to a Hudson's Bay station at Colville (100 miles north of Spokane today) to buy hoes and seed. He found that when he went anywhere, even hundreds of miles, great numbers of Indians would jump on their horses and ride along as they loved to travel, and although he was a rather thorny and opinionated man, they were fond of their Reverend Spalding—"Black Coat" was their name for him.

Hoeing was an odd activity for the Nez Perce, who would much rather do something on horseback. Out of several thousand of them who camped in the area, about seventy families helped in the cultivating, and fifteen acres were planted with potatoes and other garden vegetables, and some apple trees were set out. This was the start of food-growing in Idaho. The second year was much better because more of the Indians joined in the work. They raised wheat, barley, oats, buckwheat, corn, peas, and other garden vegetables.

Indian encampment at Lapwai.

A garden hoe was the most valuable piece of property at the mission. Mr. Spalding beat out the blades in the blacksmith shop, put handles on them, and traded them to the Indians, four hoes for one horse. Then he would take the horses to the lower Columbia River to trade them for old iron to make more hoes. The Indians valued hoes so much that they would sometimes trade each other one hoe for one horse.

The Indians also began raising a little stock—cattle, hogs and hens. Five cows, two calves and a bull had survived the hard trip from St. Louis. Mr. Spalding bought some hogs at Fort Colville, and some oxen, which had more endurance than horses. Then the mission in the Hawaiian Islands sent them five ewes and three rams, and sheep-raising, one of the great industries of Idaho, was started.

It seems odd to us that from Hawaii it was easier to reach Idaho in pioneer days, than it was from Boston. This was because of the sailing ships—they could go anywhere on the seas. On land, travel was very hard because of mountains, rivers, and hostile Indians. Boston missionaries had gone to Hawaii (which was then called the Sandwich Islands) as early as 1820, so the mission was well established before Lapwai was started. A clipper ship could sail from Hawaii right to the mouth of the Columbia River, where Dr. Whitman or Reverend Spalding could come with canoes or pack-horses to carry freight back to their missions. You can almost say that Hawaii was a neighbor to the earliest Idahoans. Your ears will tell you that our name "Owyhee" is the same word, just spelled differently. People didn't study spelling much in those days, they wrote words the way they sounded to them.

Mr. Spalding was eager for a flour mill. A barrel of flour hauled from Fort Colville cost $26 by the time it reached Lapwai, and corn-meal cost $35 a barrel. These prices were almost a fortune in those days. But there didn't seem to be the right kind of granite around Lapwai to make the millstones needed to grind the grain.

Then one day a starving man staggered into the mission, and he turned out to be a skilled workman. He claimed he could build a flour mill. First he built the waterwheel that would turn the mill-stones. Then he took a three-day journey up the Clearwater River until he found the right kind of granite. He cut a great chunk of it and floated it down to the mission on a raft. He cut the millstones to their proper shape—and the mission had a flour mill! From then on, the Indians brought their grain to be ground.

Next, the mission built a sawmill. It was rainy country and houses built of adobe clay would wash down after a while into a pile of mud. With a sawmill, they could build log buildings.

There were many other activities at the mission besides farming. Mr. Spalding kept all kinds of records about the weather, birds, animals, plants, trees. And of course he and his wife started right away to learn the language of the Nez Perce.

Mrs. Spalding was a wonderful teacher, and the Nez Perce were very intelligent and quick to learn. There were no books, so she printed books for beginners, with a pen. She taught children and their grandmothers, mothers with papooses on their backs, and gig-gling young girls. She had had a few classes in painting in Boston, and she made pictures of Bible stories to help the Indians understand. She taught the women to sew and keep house, and Mr. Spalding built a spinning wheel so she could teach them to spin the sheep wool into thread. He made a loom too, and the women wove cloth for dresses and carpeting. The young girls learned to knit; they liked to knit stockings and leggings in gay colors. Reverend Spalding loved music. He translated hymns into Nez Perce, and taught the Indians to sing.

The Hawaiian mission sent a printing press as a gift to Lapwai, a very wonderful thing for them to have. Now they could print school books, and Reverend Spalding translated parts of the Bible into Nez Perce and printed them. This was the first printing press in the whole Northwest. You can see it now, in the Oregon Historical Museum in Portland.

All of this work continued for eleven years, and then came to a sudden, tragic end.

Indians all over the country had been growing more and more upset about white settlers coming to live on their land. Dr. Whitman had promised them that the Indians would be paid for lands the white men took over, but Congress didn't appropriate any money, and the Indians were not paid. When Dr. Whitman made a journey to Boston in 1843, he didn't succeed in getting anything done about the payment. Besides that failure to help the Indians with their grievances, when Dr. Whitman returned west, an emigrant train of 1,000 new settlers came with him. Larger emigrant trains followed in the next years. The Oregon Trail cut across the hunting grounds of the Cayuse Indians, who never had been as friendly to the whites as the Nez Perce. There were trappers and fur traders around, too, who didn't want the country settled, and they egged on the hotheaded young Indians. After several years of increasing trouble, hatred burst into violence.

A group of young Cayuse Indians murdered the Whitman family at the mission near Walla Walla. Then they started for the Lapwai mission to wipe out the Spaldings. Warned by a Catholic missionary, the Spaldings escaped with their lives, but the mission was completely destroyed.

The mission board at Boston decided Idaho was too far away to be protected when the Indians went on the warpath, and they voted not to rebuild the Lapwai mission.

So ended the first farming settlement in the area that is now Idaho.

Chapter 7

CATALDO MISSION

O UR REVOLUTION in 1776 brought to an end the American Colonies of England, and the United States of America was born. So in 1976 the nation would be all set for its 200th birthday, its Bicentennial celebration.

In honor of this birthday, all the states worked out special projects. Idaho's most ambitious project was the restoration of the Cataldo Mission, the oldest building standing in our state, and one of two Idaho buildings (the other is the Assay Office) that are National Landmarks.

Its real name is the Coeur d'Alene Mission of the Sacred Heart, but it has come to be popularly known by the name of the nearby town, Cataldo. The well-loved Reverend Joseph Cataldo arrived in the area when the mission was already 13 years old, to build other missions in the Northwest. In 1877 he became Superior of all Rocky Mountain Catholic missions and made his headquarters at the Sacred Heart Mission. In his honor was named the little station a mile away on the Union Pacific Railroad where the boats landed to bring supplies for the Coeur d'Alene mines. Gradually people began to identify the mission by the name of the town.

The Jesuit fathers started the mission with the same practical intentions that inspired the Reverend Henry Spalding to found the protestant mission at Lapwai eighty miles south, twelve years earlier—to persuade the Indians to learn farming, for a more plentiful life. Attached to the mission was 600 acres of meadow and 160 acres of timber. Here, many of the Coeur d'Alenes did learn to grow potatoes and wheat, grind the wheat into flour, set out orchards, and raise livestock.

They also learned carpentry and built a church. About halfway between the present towns of Kellogg and Coeur d'Alene, it stands on a knoll high above the Coeur d'Alene river, with a sweeping view down the slopes toward river and valley.

It is wonderful to think about the building of that church. Miners had not yet arrived on the scene to blaze trails, and it would be seven or eight years before Captain John Mullan's men would chop, dig and dynamite a rough army road through the forested mountains in that area. What materials the builders did not have, they must contrive.

Cataldo Mission, outside.

That many-talented man, Father Anthony Ravalli, designed the building and drew the plans. He also carved statues with a pen-knife, made ornaments of wood and tin and paper, and directed construction. But the Coeur d'Alene Indians, untrained in the white man's kind of building, built the church. Their tools consisted of a broadax to cut down trees, a two-man crosscut saw to saw the trees into boards, a wood-boring auger to bore holes for the pegs they would make in place of nails. They had never used these tools before—yet, there stands their church, 90 feet long, 40 feet wide, and 40 feet high. Six round, smooth wooden columns support a portico of classic dignity. By any standards, it is an impressive building.

For the interior walls, since they did not have plaster, they tied willow saplings together, wove them tightly with wild grass, and packed them with mud. Fingerprints of the workers still show in this mud covering.

Some of the walls were covered with printed calico cloth to look like the mosaic work in European churches. Brother Huybrechts painstakingly carved with a pen-knife nine large and eight small panels for the ceiling, each panel a different design. The altar was made of wood, painted to look like stone. The missionaries had brought lead base to make paint, but paint colors they made from plants growing in the countryside. Lanterns and pictures were hung by leather cords. In later years, a few treasures were brought from Europe to hang in the church: pictures of Heaven and Hell, the Stations of the Cross, a biblical tapestry.

When the U.S. Government set the boundaries of the reservation for the Coeur d'Alene Indians in 1877, they did not include the area where the church was. The tribe was moved to DeSmet, about sixty miles southwest of Cataldo, where Father Peter DeSmet had built a mission in 1842.

With no one to care for it, the Coeur d'Alene mission began to deteriorate. A little repair was done in 1928, but from then on, the building suffered steadily from time, the weather, and vandals.

The Bicentennial work of restoration was paid for by money raised in Idaho, matched by money from the U.S. Government.

The restoration methods were almost as fascinating to think about as the original construction. The man hired to direct the work was Geoffrey Fairfax, a Honolulu architect who specialized in restor-

Cataldo Mission, inside.
Courtesy Idaho Historical Society

ation work. (Also for the Bicentennial, he directed the restoration of the Iolani Palace in Hawaii, the only royal palace on United States soil.) He was determined to restore the Cataldo Mission as nearly as possible to its original state.

It took real detective work. A team of archaeologists from the University of Idaho spent a season gathering information at the site. Other teams researched old records of the Jesuit missionaries in the Crosby Library at Gonzaga University at Spokane. Paint and adobe samples were sent to New York University to be analyzed for what information of the past they could give. Teams on the project included Coeur d'Alene Indians, Jesuit priests, engineers, local architects, and student archaeologists. Mr. Fairfax wanted to have as many Idahoans as possible work with his specialists, to gather training to apply to the restoration of other historical Idaho buildings.

The mission had settled and sagged, and a complete new rock foundation had to be laid in under the structure. The west wall had bulged out and had to be replaced. The six white columns supporting the front portico had become decrepit and were rebuilt. When a stronger foundation was being laid, the whole front of the church was removed, each piece being numbered so they could be reassembled again exactly in their original positions.

An interesting hole was left in the wall behind the altar to allow visitors to see how the wall was constructed of willows, grass and mud.

For two years the whole outside of the building was latticed with scaffolding, and young workers ran up and down ladders, and in the backyard measured and sawed and fitted boards supported on sawhorses, so busy and absorbed, they never looked up at the tourists wandering around.

Surely it would warm the hearts of those pioneer builders to see with what appreciation and respect today's generation works to preserve the labor their forebears achieved in a wilderness.

Chapter 8

FRANKLIN, IN IDAHO

A FTER THE MORMONS had settled the valleys near Salt Lake, Brigham Young called on groups of families to leave their homes and pioneer farther away. On April 14, 1860, twenty-three families drove their wagons to the north end of Cache Valley and halted on what was to be Main Street of Franklin —first town in Idaho. They thought they were still in Utah; but they had just crossed over the boundary into Idaho country.

They took the canvas-covered wagon boxes off their frames and arranged them in the shape of a fort, to live in till they had time to build cabins. First they must clear and cultivate the ground and plant vegetables and grain. Several children were born in the wagon box homes that first summer. And all summer more emigrants came driving in, until there were sixty families living in Franklin.

The men built roads to the wooded canyons, cut logs, and hauled them back to town on the wagon frames. The cabins they built were exactly alike. There was a fireplace at one end to cook in and to give heat and light. The floor and roof were packed dirt, and when it rained, the roof leaked mud. The housewives had to put up with mud in their hair for ten years before a mill was built to make shingles.

The cabins faced toward the center, so that their outside walls formed a fort. Inside was a corral to protect the stock from Indians and wild animals at night, and a well where everybody brought their buckets for water. You can see a replica of this fort today, in the Relic Hall at Franklin.

They found out right away that it was too dry to raise crops without extra water. With picks and shovels the men dug a ditch 3½ miles long, to bring water from Maple Creek Canyon.

Twenty children started classes in one of the cabins, but within the first year a schoolhouse was built. Like the homes, the schoolhouse had a fireplace at one end, and a dirt floor and roof, and probably the children giggled when the mud dripped on their heads; but the school-house had something that the homes didn't have, something of which they were very proud—three small windows, the glass panes brought all the way from Salt Lake City. There was only one spelling book for the whole school, but each class had a reader. Someone found slate deposits up in the mountains, and made the slabs into slates and slate pencils for the school.

The schoolhouse was used for meetings too, and for church and dances. These hard-working, very religious people, loved a good time too. A few years before, many of them had walked the 1300 miles from Iowa City to Salt Lake, pulling everything they owned in a handcart, and you would think that by night they would only want to sleep; but no, they would gather around the campfires and dance half the night among the sagebrush. And now in Franklin, they watered down the dirt floor in the schoolhouse, the fiddlers tuned up, the caller yodeled, and mothers, fathers and children all began to stomp and swing.

Even their work they could sometimes make into fun. The women would bring all their spinning wheels to one home, and race to see who could spin the most yarn, laughing and visiting as their fingers flew. When the boys went to the canyons to cut wood, the girls went along to pick berries to be dried for winter, and they had a jolly picnic lunch and all rode home together on the wagonload of wood.

The women made dyes for cloth from berries and plants and tree bark, and they wove hats from wheat and oat straw.

Brigham Young sent them a 10,000-pound steam engine from the East. It went up the Missouri River on a boat, then by wagon hundreds of miles over the mountains. This precious machine ran the colony's sawmill. You can see it today in the Franklin Relic Hall. They also built a flour mill. The turbine wheel that the creek water turned to rotate the stone to grind the wheat, was sent out from the East, but the stone was Utah granite.

Cache Valley had for generations been a winter camping place for Indians, and they outnumbered the settlers by many hundreds. Franklin men took turns acting as lookout on Little Mountain (called Mount Lookout today) just in case, but the settlers really believed they could get along with the Indians. Most white pioneers thought "the only good Indian was a dead Indian," but the Mormons didn't think that way. Their religion regarded Indians as a branch of the Children of Israel in the Bible. Brigham Young always urged his people to feed the Indians and try to be helpful to them.

This system didn't work out as well as expected. The Indians began to come every day for grain and flour, and the settlers had barely enough for themselves. By mid-winter, supplies were so low that some of the men had to walk the 110 miles to Salt Lake, and carry fifty-pound sacks of flour home on their backs. By then the settlers at Franklin were living on sago root and boiled wheat. And still the Indians came, demanding more.

In 1862, a band of Cache Valley Shoshoni arrived to winter on the Bear River twelve miles from Franklin. It was a band dedicated to discouraging whites from taking over Indian country, and they had spent a busy autumn fighting and burning emigrant trains. Now, from their winter quarters, they began to harass the settlement at Franklin with increased demands for grain and flour, running off cattle and stealing tools. The settlers became very nervous about venturing outside the walls of their fort.

The climax came in December. Some miners (who were not Mormons) driving their wagons down from their mine near Leesburg, to Salt Lake City for supplies, became lost in a snowstorm and drove near the Indian camp. The Indians attacked them, burning the wagons, killing one man and wounding several others.

Emboldened by this success, some of the warriors then rode their horses to Franklin and demanded 24 bushels of flour. There seemed to be nothing to do but give it to them. Then the Indians demanded more. The settlers now became stubborn and refused. The Indians began a war dance, whooping around and waving their tomahawks until the settlers were terrified. Finally the Indians rode away, but next day Chief Bear Hunter and some Indian women were back for more grain.

While the grain was being poured into sacks, a company of infantry came marching in from Salt Lake. One of the wounded miners had made it through and gotten the word to Fort Douglas, and the commander had decided that action couldn't wait on the weather; the way things were going, the settlers weren't going to be able to hold out.

It was bitter cold and most of the soldiers were suffering frostbite from the long march. At three o'clock in the morning, a small number of cavalry arrived, and with the foot soldiers, started off through the heavy snow for the Indian camp on Bear River.

The Franklin men set themselves to guard the fort as best they could. They placed themselves in a line from Franklin to the top of a hill overlooking Bear River where the battle would take place, so they could signal the news of how it was going, from one to another back along the line to Franklin.

A marker stands where U.S. Highway 91 crosses Battle Creek, to recall that terrible battle of January, 1863.

The soldiers arrived at Bear River at dawn. The Indians, warned by Chief Bear Hunter that soldiers had arrived at Franklin, were hidden in a wide, brushy ravine, a perfect natural defense. The cavalry swept down the hill and across the river. Heavy gunfire from the Indians drove them back. They re-formed and charged again, and again they were driven back. A third time they charged, and still the bullets were too deadly for them. The terrifying news of these retreats was relayed back along the line of men, and the women and children barricaded in the Franklin schoolhouse believed their last day had come.

But after that third retreat, the soldiers divided into three parties. One worked its way around and up the ravine, one came down the ravine, and one attacked from the front. This brought the soldiers and the Indians into hand-to-hand combat. The slaughter raged for two hours, the soldiers with bayonets, the Indians (men, women and children battling for survival) with knives and tomahawks. The soldiers were soaking wet from crossing the river, and when they fell wounded, they froze to death.

When it was over, many soldiers were dead and wounded, but the Indians were almost annihilated. Dr. Merle Wells, historian, says this is believed to have been the most destructive battle suffered by Indians in U.S. history. Around 400 of them were involved, at least half of whom were women and children, and when it was over there were almost none left. A few managed to escape during the fighting. A few wounded women and children who survived, were taken to Franklin and nursed back to health. Two Indian orphans were raised by Franklin familes.

The terrible results made a deep impression on Indians everywhere, and put an end to serious troubles with them in that section. The whites were beginning to outnumber Indians. The settlement of Franklin would survive.

Chapter 9

INITIAL POINT

WHEN A NEW country is settled, one of the first things the government does is start a survey of the land so that settlers can prove where their boundaries are. George Washington learned the basics of surveying 57 years before he would become our first President. He practiced his new-learned skill by plotting and measuring the Virginia fields of his brothers and neighbors. When he was 17 he became Public Surveyor for Fairfax County, Virginia, and his work of surveying along the edge of the wilderness west, of that time, whetted his interest in our western lands, an interest that would last through his lifetime.

In 1863, Idaho was organized as a Territory. A few years later the survey of its lands was begun. How would you start surveying 53,476,480 acres of untouched land? If you would like to see where Idaho did start, drive out the road south of Kuna that leads to the old Swan Falls power plant on the Snake River. Eight miles south of Kuna you will see a volcanic butte rising out of the sagebrush plain over to the east. It looks like some huge old animal sleeping, one of the kind that has been extinct for a few million years. It has a knob at the top of its head, and on the knob seems to be perched a little crown.

Take a side road through the sagebrush, and drive steeply up around the butte. You will have to walk the last little way, and climb a dozen steps to the knob. Then you see that what looked like a crown from a long way off, is really a railing to keep people from tumbling off.

You are standing on the cliff side of the butte. You look in every direction, and there is not a house in sight, not a car, nor a man, nor a horse, nor a cow. Miles and miles and miles of sagebrush and space. It's what the man meant who said, "You can see from here to eternity."

Bring your gaze back from distance, and under your feet you will find a brass cap. This marks Idaho's "Initial Point," the starting point for measuring all the land in Idaho. It was established on April 19, 1867, by Peter W. Bell by order of Surveyor General Lafayette Cartee.

Peter Bell, by astronomical observations, surveyed a Boise Meridian Line, exactly north and south through this point. (The

Initial Point.
Courtesy, U.S. Bureau of Land Management

town of Meridian was given its name because it sits on the Boise Meridian Line, exactly north of Initial Point.) At right angles to the meridian line, he surveyed the east-west Boise Base Line through the Initial Point. Along both these lines he began measuring off the land into squares with six-mile sides, called Townships, and each township into 36 little squares with one-mile sides, called Sections (a section has 640 acres.)

This is the language of land description, which doesn't speak in terms of miles. Instead it says a piece of land is so many Townships north or south of Initial Point, and so many Ranges east or west of Initial Point. A "Range" is a six-mile square just as a township is, but range is used to describe east or west distance from Initial Point, while township describes north or south distance from it.

If a man tells you his land is in Sec. 1, T.2S., R.2W., B.M., he means it is in Section 1, of the second Township south, and the second Range west, from Initial Point. Boise Meridian ("B.M.") identifies the description as applying to Idaho land.

It seems a very interesting thing to me that every piece of land in Idaho, whether it is in the bottom of Hells Canyon, or on top of

12,662-foot Mt. Borah, or the block where our capitol building stands, or the lot where my own house is built, is located on a land map by its distance and direction from that little brass cap out in the sagebrush, Initial Point.

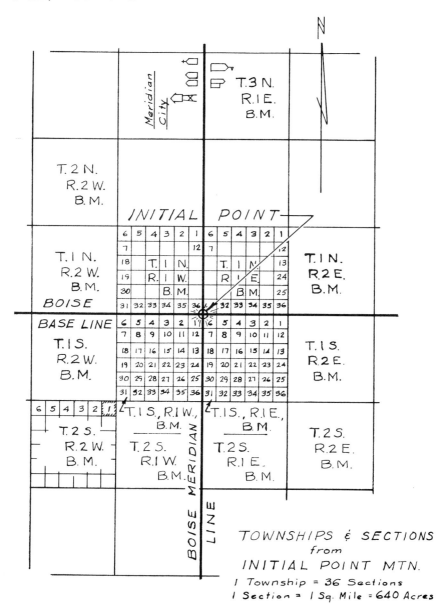

Land surveys from Initial Point.

Drawing by Robt. P. Newell

Part of an Urquides pack train in a 1913 Boise parade.

Courtesy Idaho Historical Society

Chapter 10

FROM HERE TO THERE

EXCEPT FOR IRRIGATION, the way of life in Idaho has been most changed by the difference in travel and communication. Housing, heat, lights and plumbing are a whole lot more convenient than they used to be, but they don't change all our plans and activities.

In the beginning, animals made trails when they were hunting berries, roots, pasture and water. Indians followed the trails, marking them more deeply. White men came, following the Indian trails; Lewis and Clark, fur traders, missionaries, miners and finally, settlers.

Up north, the Nez Perce trail called the Lolo, crossed the state from Lewiston to Montana. Our Lewis and Clark Highway, U.S. 12, follows it closely.

In the south, the Bannock and Shoshoni trail that we came to call the Old Oregon Trail, crossed Idaho from Wyoming to Oregon. This was the route of the settlers on their way to the green valleys of Oregon and California. From the 1840's to the 1890's, thousands of settlers came this way, hundreds of wagon trains, wheels cutting deeper and deeper, so that now, after nearly a century, the ruts can still be seen. This was the road that made it possible for Americans to reach Oregon and Washington before the British should decide to bring their people by ship. The whole Northwest finally became the property of the United States by reason of settlement.

Across the narrow panhandle, in 1859, Captain John Mullan's men dug and chopped and dynamited an Army road for soldiers and equipment to travel the 624 miles from Fort Benton, Montana to Fort Walla Walla, in times of Indian trouble. This is the Mullan Highway, our U.S. 10, that passes Coeur d'Alene and the Cataldo Mission. You may have seen the historical Mullan Tree, marked in Fourth of July Canyon. The canyon got its name when the road builders celebrated the Fourth by shooting off a lot of gunpowder in carbine and cannon, sending the Coeur d'Alene Indians fleeing for the mission.

Our first white men walked or came on horseback. With the discovery of gold and silver, came the pack mules. From 1861, steamboats came up the Snake River bringing cargos to Lewiston, from where they were packed to the mines by mule train. A steamboat could go up the Coeur d'Alene River to near the Cataldo Mission, taking supplies that would go on from there to the mines by mule back.

The names best-known to us in packing in Idaho are Packer John Welch, and the Spaniard, Jesus Urquides (pronounced "Hay-soos Ur-keed-is".)

Packer John headquartered at Lewiston and packed to both the northern and the southern mining camps. His trails would eventually become our North-and-South Highway, U.S. 95.

One year Packer John's train was caught in a blizzard on its way south to the Boise Basin mines, and could not proceed. Near where New Meadows is now, the men felled lodgepole pine and built a storage cabin to keep dry the supplies they were carrying, until spring, then took the mules back to Lewiston for the winter. This little cabin, being about halfway between the two largest settlements, was used for several early Territorial political conventions, although it must have been something like holding a meeting in a telephone booth. The cabin has been restored, and if you have a few minutes to spare the next time you come to the historical marker on the highway, you can turn off and drive the short distance into the forest to see it.

A few miles south of Smith's Ferry there is a mountain ridge named for Packer John, and a forest lookout.

Jesus Urquides, whose name is Basque, although he always called himself a Spaniard, was perhaps the most famous and respected packer in the West, where he packed for more than sixty years. Not long after Colonel Pinckney Lugenbeel rode in with his cavalry to establish the military post at Boise to protect the settlers, and lay out the town, Jesus Urquides built his little "Urquides Village" (later known as "Spanish Village"), in the cottonwoods at the spot where Main Street changes to Warm Springs Avenue. He built a cottage for himself, thirty cabins and a cookshack for his drivers, and storehouses, corrals and stables. Those thirty little cabins, hidden away behind Boise's most fashionable street, were used for more than 100 years, first by his employees, and later by old pensioners who had no family and no other place to live. They were finally cleared away in 1973 because of the fire hazard.

Pack trains carried everything. Mining equipment, steel cables, the makings of sawmills and flour mills, furniture, sacks of ore, cantinas of gold dust, bags and bales and barrels of food for the thousands of people in the mining camps. They even transported pianos to the saloons and gambling houses—in a canvas case, the piano was slung between four mules. In all his years of packing,

Urquides' daughter, Lola Dolores Binnard, said her father was robbed only once, when Indians got away with a train of 75 mules. Urquides died in 1928, at the age of 96. When I was a little girl, he used to ride in Boise parades. When we heard the harness bells jingling, all the children would shout, "Here comes the pack train!" and at the head of it, very trim and erect would come riding the plump, little old gentleman with his neat white goatee, looking like a Spanish grandee.

One odd item in our packing history was the appearance, for a short while, of a string of camels. The Army had been experimenting with their use in the Southwest deserts, and some enterprising packer bought them up. They weren't practical on our narrow mountain trails as they scared mules and horses out their wits, sending them stampeding down the mountains. You can imagine the fate of a piano if its four pack-mules should come around a corner and meet a string of the weird-looking beasts face to face.

Trails became worn wider until a wagon could travel them. Hustling young men built toll roads and bridges and ferries and made themselves a lot of money. (The toll station on the Harris Creek road at the busy period of the Boise Basin mines was said to take in a thousand dollars a day.) Freighters took over the business of the mule trains, hitching wagons together and harnessing long strings of oxen, mules or horses.

The pioneer in the freight business we remember best is John Hailey. He had also been in the packing and saddle-train lines, meeting the steamboat at Umatilla, Oregon, three times a week and carrying supplies over the hills to the Boise Basin.

John Hailey was an example of our best type of pioneer; intelligent, enterprising, energetic, adaptable and a good citizen. Until he was 18, he worked on farms in Tennessee and Missouri, and had a few years of country schooling. In 1853, he drove a five-yoke oxteam across the country from Missouri to Oregon, where he farmed, raised stock, did some packing, and took part in an Indian war. After his packing and freighting days, he started a stage line, and took part in Idaho's early political activities, serving two terms as territorial delegate in Congress. At the request of our legislature, he wrote the first complete history of Idaho, in which he stated in his modest way, "I knew but little when I started out to do for myself. I have been trying to learn something ever since, but find that I know but little now; but I remember most all I have seen or learned." Our town of Hailey, of course, was named for him.

People who had left their homes in the East to strike out for themselves, never expecting to see their families again, were terribly homesick for news from home. What few letters came, were passed along from one traveler to another in the hope they would finally reach the people for whom they were intended.

In 1861, one of the most colorful experiments of our history was undertaken in the Pony Express. Twenty-five mile relays of sturdy saddle horses covered the 2,000 miles from St. Joseph, Missouri, to Sacramento, California, in ten or eleven days. It was a grueling trip, what with mountains, rivers, salt flats, storms and hostile Indians, and after seven months it was more than $100,000 in the red. The experiment died a quick death, but for those few months the mail crossed the United States in a cloud of dust like a whirlwind.

The emigrants were coming across the continent now, in their canvas-covered Conestoga wagons, on their way to the green Willamette Valley in Oregon. Not one of them was tempted to stay in Idaho, that vast plain of sagebrush they plodded through.

Ben Holladay and the other "Stagecoach Kings" were stirring themselves. Mark Twain said, "Everybody has heard of Ben Holladay, who sent the mails and passengers flying across the continent, two thousand miles in fifteen days, by the watch!" Mark Twain, himself, rode west in a Concord stagecoach in 1861, and gives us a

Union Pacific train at McCammon, Idaho.

Courtesy Idaho Historical Society

wonderfully entertaining account of the trip in his book, "Roughing It." He also described a trip he took to the Holy Land years later, and of listening to a guide tell about the forty-year ordeal of Moses bringing the Children of Israel across the desert from Egypt to the Promised Land. "Forty years!" cried a young chap who had traveled in our Far West. "Only three hundred miles? Ben Holladay would have fetched them through in thirty-six hours!"

Idaho's first telegraph was hooked up in a co-operative store in Franklin in 1868, and our first telephone was installed at Hailey in 1883 when the Hailey country was having its mining boom.

But first came the railroad. In 1869 the Golden Spike, completing the transcontinental railroad, was pounded in at Promontory Summit in Utah, where the Union Pacific tracks arrived from the east, and the Central Pacific tracks from the west.

The railroad wasn't routed through Salt Lake, so the Mormon Church organized its own local companies to build connecting lines to several Mormon settlements. One of these was Franklin, Idaho, introducing the first railroad to Idaho. Mormon farmers along the route did the grading and furnished ties, taking stock in the company for pay. The railroad building of these strict-living families was accompanied by family prayers, blessings on meals, Sunday rest, and fresh milk from the herd they brought along with them; a startling contrast to the traditions of the usual "Hell on Wheels" railroad crews whose work was accompanied by much whisky, tea, opium, and general hell-raising. The Mormons built hardly more than half a mile a day, but worked steadily along until completion in 1874.

The narrow-gauge (three feet wide) tracks took less fill and grading, and cost less than half as much as standard-gauge (about 4-2/3 feet wide). Four years later the Union Pacific extended this narrow-gauge line from Franklin north to Garrison, Montana to serve the mines there. A few years later the Oregon Short Line built an east-west line that was standard-gauge across southern Idaho, and the difference in track widths caused a complicated problem when shipments were rerouted from one line to the other. A car had to be lifted from one set of wheels to another, and some of these car-loads proved too heavy for the little narrow-gauge locomotives, which were less than thirty feet long. When they were replaced with heavier locomotives, some of the curves gave way under their weight. Gradually the roadbed was strengthened, and finally, on July 24, 1887, the narrow tracks were replaced by standard width in a striking demonstration of American efficiency at its best. On that morning, gangs were stationed along the 262 miles of track between Franklin and Garrison, each to complete one section. The job was finished by mid-afternoon, the train not having missed a single schedule! So ended the era of our rough-riding single-gauge "galloping gooses."

The east-west railroad mentioned above was built by the Oregon Short Line in 1884 from Granger, Wyoming to Huntington, Oregon. When it was completed, it ran a special excursion (one day), the 340 miles from Pocatello to Payette.

Charlie Walgamott, Twin Falls pioneer, makes an entertaining yarn of the event in his book of reminiscences, "Six Decades Back." He said the special train carried railroad officials, one hundred tourists, and the Silver Cornet Band from Ogden, Utah. The excursion had been widely advertised, and for 75 miles around, families got up at dawn and into their wagons, and cowboys onto their horses, and rode to American Falls to see the train and hear the Silver Cornet Band.They arrived and looked over the tiny new station long before the train was due to arrive. When the whistle finally blew and the train came chugging along, the families and cowboys cleared off the station platform so the band could use it, and they formed into a big circle of eager expectation.

But something was wrong with those passengers; they must have been stuffed shirts from the city, not about to notice the country folk. They didn't respond with so much as a wave of the hand, and the band members did not unpack their horns.

Our pioneers, who had ridden so many hours for their treat, were astounded. Then the cowboys, not known for their long patience, got mad. Pulling their guns, they marched into the train and led out the band. One of the railroad men rushed forward to the engine to urge the engineer and fireman to get going, only to find that the engine crew was also being held at gunpoint.

The Ogden Silver Cornet Band began to play. Mr. Walgamott reported in his reminiscences that they played a nervous, syncopated rhythm "later known as jazz." The cowboys brought beer and soft drinks from the saloon, and the passengers gradually became more human.When the train was at last allowed to proceed, the good-natured engineer toot-tooted long and shrilly, and the cowboys fired volley after volley into the sky, before they turned their horses and started happily home again.

The airlines arrived in Idaho in 1926. And the rest, you know.

First airmail flight in Idaho, Boise, April 6, 1926. Leon Cuddeback, pilot. Senator Borah in foreground.

Courtesy Idaho Historical Society

Chinese miners washing gold with rockers.

Chapter 11

CHINESE IN IDAHO

T HERE ARE VERY few Chinese in Idaho today, but in the 1870 census 4300 were counted. That was nearly one-third of Idaho's total population of that time.

When news of the discovery of gold in California in 1848 went like a wind around the world, men came by the shipload from nearly every nation to try to get a little share of the precious stuff. From China, where millions of coolies never had enough to eat, they came by the hundreds, many of them young boys, sailing on the last of the clipper ships. They plodded up and down the California gulches, trying to shake a few grains of gold out of a pan of gravel and water. And when the gold began to run out in California, they walked up the coast and east to Idaho, where new gold strikes had been made in the north part of the state.

A few years later, when the Civil War ended, the nation went to work to build a railroad from the Atlantic Ocean to the Pacific Ocean. The West was becoming an important part of the country, and men needed a quicker way to reach it. The United States was still too young to have enough workers of its own for such a tremendous project, so it invited immigrants to come and work on the railroad. On the Atlantic side, men came over from Ireland, where there had been a potato blight and people were starving to death. And on the Pacific Coast, the Chinese came.

Americans didn't like the Chinese. Coolies would work for very low pay, and that made wages lower for everybody. They didn't intend to make America their permanent home either, they just wanted to save a few hundred dollars and take it back to China. But the main reason Americans didn't like them, was because they were different. They looked different, they had slanted eyes and a pigtail braid, and they wore clothes like pajamas. They didn't speak like Americans, they spoke Chinese, very strange-sounding indeed. They ate different things than Americans did. They lived by themselves. People don't like other people to be different.

But later, when Chinese turned from mining or the railroad, and started laundries and restaurants and shops, or cooked for a family, Americans began to get acquainted with them. In business the Chinese had to be able to talk to other people, and they worked out a simple language that anybody could understand. It was called "pidgin English." "Pidgin" was the nearest a Chinese could come to saying "business." That's what this simple language was, "business English"—words a Chinese could use doing business with Americans. And when they could talk to each other, sure enough, some of them began to like each other. Americans found most Chinese to be good-natured, patient, hard-working people, with a great sense of humor.

But when thousands of Chinese were mining, or working on the railroad, Americans simply didn't consider them human beings. The Chinese had no legal rights in this country. If you have ever noticed a flock of chickens, when one is weak and can't protect itself, the other chickens will pick on it. That is the way it was with the un-protected Chinese in this country, bullies found it was safe to pick on them because they couldn't hit back. Even children tormented them, following the example of the grown-ups. They would roll rocks down hills to break windows in Chinese buildings. They would climb to a rooftop and plug up the stovepipe so the house filled with smoke. Great joke.

The coolies were mistreated even more by their own people, the rich Chinese merchants of San Francisco. The merchants formed companies to pay the coolies' fare from China. Then they set up gambling houses and opium dens to try to win back all the money the coolies could earn.

White miners made the mining camp laws, which in early days was about all the law we had in the West. They passed a law saying that a Chinese couldn't own a mining claim. Then when the gold began to peter out, they changed the law so that Americans could sell their worn-out claims to the Chinese and get a few more hundred dollars. The Chinese were so painstaking that they were able to scrape out a living from the washed-over gravels. Then sometimes the white men, having poor luck in other places, would come back and "jump" the claims, pulling a gun on the Chinese. A Chinese didn't dare defend himself; any court would hang him.

The Idaho Legislature passed a law that a Chinese had to pay a tax of four dollars a month to be allowed to work as a miner. Then it was increased to five dollars a month. The sheriff collected this tax, and one dollar of it belonged to him. You would know that there would be ornery, fast-buck loafers around, who would show a blank notice to a Chinese miner (who of course couldn't read English), and tell him they had been deputized by the sheriff to collect the tax. Later the real sheriff would come around and collect again. You have heard people say, "He doesn't have a chinaman's chance." That expression came straight out of Idaho's early history.

Idahoans mistreated these people shamefully and long; but sometimes we are jolted out of our bad habits in spite of ourselves. It

Chinese vegetable peddler at Idaho City.

is a surprising fact that in 1869, the first legal hanging in southern Idaho, was a white man convicted of killing a harmless Chinese.

The Chinese was a passenger on a freight wagon camped overnight by the Payette River. Wrapped in his blanket, he lay asleep on the ground beside the wagon. Anthony McBride, an Irish laborer, happened by. He was drunk, and he may have been a little crazy to begin with. He asked a bystander whether the man sleeping in the blanket was a Chinaman or an Indian, and when the man answered, "A Chinaman," McBride pulled out a pistol, said, "Well I'll just shoot him for luck," and fired into the blanket.

McBride was arrested, not so much because he had killed a Chinese as because he was a dangerous, crazy fellow to have around, but the surprising outcome was that a jury of white men found him guilty of cold-blooded murder, and a white judge sentenced him to be hanged. Dick d'Easum, author of Idaho historical articles in the Idaho Statesman newspaper, drew an interesting conclusion from this trial: this judge and this jury were admitting, for the first time in Idaho's legal history, that a Chinese is a human being, one of the "all men are created equal" of our Declaration of Independence, and as such, to be protected by the laws of our nation.

Chapter 12

THE CAPTAIN OF
THE PAYETTE VIGILANTES

I N NOVEMBER, 1974, the 104th birthday of Mary Borah, widow of Senator William Borah, was noted in the newspapers. It made me realize that all of Idaho's history since the gold rush has taken place in one lifetime.

It also started me remembering Mrs. Borah's father, dynamic and colorful William J. McConnell. Mr. McConnell was a prominent public figure for sixty years, but his most fascinating exploits for a reader occurred when, at the age of 25, he became Captain of the Payette Vigilantes.

Billy McConnell grew up in Michigan, an itchy-footed boy who could scarcely wait to be old enough to go out West where all that gold and excitement waited.

In 1860, when he was 21, he started west as one of the drivers of a mule train to be sold in California. It was a lively trip. On the same day the mules started from Atchison, Kansas, the first pony express rider started out from St. Joseph, Missouri, bound for Sacramento. Their paths soon came together and the mules stampeded, causing a lot of trouble before they were brought under control. Also, the Indians were on the warpath, and after the last settlement, signal fires began to flare on every nearby mountain. The train clashed with Indian bands in several rocky canyons, but the mules were at last brought safely through.

Schoolteachers were scarce in the West, and McConnell intended to get a job teaching in California, but things were so lively in Virginia City, Nevada, that he got side-tracked. He worked at a lot of different jobs, and like everybody else, he hunted for gold. But gold was running out in Nevada and California and after a while he went on to Oregon and did teach school. Then in 1863, the Boise Basin gold discoveries exploded on the world, and that was where young McConnell had to be. He went up the Columbia River by boat and rode overland with a pack train.

In the spring of 1863, the Boise Basin was going great guns. Placerville, Centerville, Pioneerville, Quartzburg, and Idaho City (then known as Bannock) were well supplied with saloons, hotels and restaurants.

Billy McConnell, age 25, 1864.

Photo from McConnell's "Early History of Idaho."
Courtesy Idaho Historical Society

In California, McConnell had discovered that men who raised truck gardens in the neighborhood of the mines, did better financially than men who hunted for gold. Here were 30,000 hungry men. All goods and supplies came from Portland, brought by boat up the Columbia River to Umatilla Landing, Oregon, then overland by pack mule or wagon. It made everything terribly expensive. McConnell found a sunny location in Jerusalem Valley on Jerusalem creek above Horseshoe Bend, and he and a partner went to work raising vegetables. They started by planting two gallons of onion sets. The soil was rich; the onions grew in a hurry. In a month the young gardeners pulled the crop, tied them in bunches of a dozen each, packed them over the hills to Placerville, and sold them as fast as they could hand them out—one hundred bunches at a dollar a bunch. The first green vegetables sold in Boise Basin.

But although the vegetables grew and sold fabulously, there was, as usual, a serpent in the garden. Wherever there is gold, thieves gather to share it. They robbed, they murdered, they passed bogus gold, and most of all, they stole horses and mules and cows.

It is hard for us today to understand early Idahoans who had come from law-abiding communities in the East, taking the law into their own hands. Nowadays, that is regarded as one of the worst crimes. But the mining camps were so isolated from the rest of the country, and local government was so undeveloped, that laws at first could not protect the property or even the lives of ranchers and emigrants.

Three men who had been engaged in robbing stages and stealing horses and cattle in New Mexico, came to Idaho in 1863. to look over the prospects in the new gold boom. The prospects looked mighty good. Thousands of horses and mules after bringing miners to the Basin, were turned loose on the bunch grass that grew lush around Horseshoe Bend.

To round up a herd of these at night and drive them down the trail to sell in Oregon, Nevada and California, was a very profitable business. The three located their headquarters in the Emmett Valley near the entrance to the canyon leading to Horseshoe Bend. They built a log house and a corral strong enough to act as a fort. It was called the "Picket Corral," and the Picket Corral Gang became the most notorious outlaws in southern Idaho.

They located a second ranch where South Boise is now, protected from searchers by thick willows and cottonwoods and the Boise River, which in those days before dams, flowed deep, and they built a lookout tower just east of where the Broadway bridge now crosses the river. Whenever it was necessary to hold stolen stock a few days before taking them on the trail, they would bring them across the

Placerville in the Boise Basin mining area.

Lithograph, Courtesy Idaho Historical Society

hills from Horseshoe Bend to Dry Creek, detour around Boise to the river above the present Julia Davis Park, and swim them across the river to the hidden ranch.

The Picket Corral gang was made up of big, good-looking men, fine horsemen and good companions, generous to anyone in trouble and they became popular. This made it possible for them to take an active part in the first Democratic nominating convention in Ada County. In fact, because it was of special interest to their activities, crooks were about the only ones who took the time to work in local politics and government. In this way the Picket Corral gang was able to get one of their own men, Dave Opdyke, elected sheriff of Ada County. This not only protected their thievery, but in case an outlaw did happen to be arrested, it controlled the jury, since under the laws of Idaho Territory, one of the duties of the sheriff was to select the list of possible jurors from tax assessment rolls.

This was the situation when McConnell started raising vegetables and packing them over the hills to the Boise Basin. He made money beyond his fondest hopes but he lost it almost as fast, when horse thieves made nightly raids on his livestock. He put up with it for awhile because the racket seemed hopeless for one man to fight, but one day when a favorite saddle horse was missing, he couldn't take it any longer.

He rode down to Boise City and searched all the livery stables and feed corrals. He failed to find the mare he was looking for, but he did find a horse that had been stolen from him a couple of months before. The present owner wouldn't give him up. McConnell and a lawyer friend who had just started practice in the town, decided to take it to court. Poor, innocent young fellows! The justice of the peace was hand-in-glove with Sheriff Opdyke and the thieves, and before he would issue a writ, he made McConnell weigh out enough gold dust to pay all the estimated costs, including a back stable bill. It came to over seventy dollars, nearly the full value of the horse. You can imagine McConnell's helpless rage. In later years he said he entered that courtroom a green boy, and came out a grim-faced man.

When he led the horse out of the stable, half-a-dozen horse-thieves and stage-robbers were standing around, grinning. McConnell told them he would like to make them a speech. They said, "Fire away." At the end of a number of personal remarks, he stated, "I can catch any tough who rides these hills. The next man who steals a horse from me will be my injun. There won't be any lawsuit."

The outlaws were tickled at these brave words from someone they regarded as just a kid. They decided to teach the "rutabaga peddler" how to take a joke. A few nights later they raided Jerusalem

Valley, stealing five valuable horses and four large mules worth two thousand dollars.

If McConnell didn't do something now, he might just as well leave the country. He gathered a posse of four gardeners from the valley. Well-armed and each riding one good horse and leading another, they started in pursuit.

The trip was wild and adventurous, but when they returned, they didn't seem to want to talk about it. They said it was two weeks before they overtook the five thieves, asleep in their blankets in a camp near La Grande, Oregon. The posse had ridden all night, and planned to attack at daylight, but when a dog began barking, the thieves sat up and started shooting.

The posse came home to Jerusalem Valley with all their gaunt horses and mules, and said there was no need to worry any more about those particular horse thieves.

The ranchers around the Payette Valley found it very cheering to realize the outlaws were not, after all, invincible. They decided to make an organized effort to clear them out of the country.

Nearly every good citizen of the valley was present when the "Payette Vigilance Committee" was organized. Because William McConnell had proved his mettle in a contest with the outlaws, he was elected captain. The rules were simple. An accused man was entitled to a trial by jury of seven members of the Committee. A majority of this jury would render a verdict. For conviction there would be three kinds of sentence: (1) Leave the country within 24 hours. (2) Be publicly horsewhipped. (3) Be hanged.

As their first project, the Committee voted to clear out the counterfeiters who passed "bogus gold" in the area. Practically the only form of money used in the West at that time was gold dust. Counterfeiters spent a lot of time and effort scheming to get their share of it. The best "bogus gold" was manufactured in San Francisco. Lead bars were cut into tiny particles and galvanized with real gold. Without cutting into it, it could hardly be detected from the real thing. It was easy for agents to pass it off to emigrants, or use it to pay packers and teamsters for hauling freight. Another trick along the Payette Valley road was for an agent to stop at a roadhouse and ask to leave a deposit of gold dust for safekeeping for a few weeks. The bogus stuff would be weighed, a receipt given, and the counterfeit dumped into the proprietor's baking powder can, already partly full of real gold dust. By the time the agent returned to reclaim his weight of dust, additions to and withdrawals from the can in trade would have left almost pure dust.

The local agent of the bogus gold syndicate made his headquarters with the Picket Corral gang. The vigilantes appointed a committee of one to meet a five-man escort at a roadhouse near the Picket Corral at noon the next day, and proceed to serve the agent with a notice to leave the country and not come back. The lone committeeman, being some distance from his home, decided to go on to the roadhouse and spend the night. Unfortunately, at breakfast he found four Picket gang men present, including the bogus gold agent. He had a chilly feeling that the grapevine had been busy and they knew what his business was.

Sure enough, after breakfast one of them asked him to come outside. There wasn't much else he could do. He slipped his two Colt's revolvers forward on his belt and went out. The men struck up a conversation and edged him along to a small corral built of 12-inch logs set upright, close together. He understood that he was about to be quietly murdered without witnesses. His five-man escort wasn't due for hours. Quickly sizing up his chances, he decided to take as many of the gang with him as possible. The instant he was edged into the corral, he backed into a corner against the logs and announced that if one of them reached for a gun, there would be the biggest funeral ever held in the Payette Valley. The surprised gunmen, who had thought this was going to be easy, were thrown off their stride, and a heated discussion followed. The vigilante tried to serve his notice; the agent refused to accept it. Keeping a sharp eye on the gunmen, the vigilante read it aloud. A lot of hot words and haranguing followed, but in the end the strongest character triumphed. The bogus gold agent did arrange his affairs and leave the country the next day. The syndicate called off its operations in that area.

This success of ordinary citizens worried other outlaws. It made them mad, too. Two brothers who owned the Washoe Ferry on the Oregon side of the Snake River near Payette, and were well-known to harbor criminals, sent an insulting letter to the Committee with copies to mining towns around the country, challenging the Committee to try to take the ferry-house. This house was practically a fort, built to withstand Indian attacks. It had no windows, only gun-holes, and a dirt roof that couldn't be set afire.

The vigilance committee discussed the many crimes and outlaws connected with the ferry, and decided to take up the challenge.

Twenty men rode out one afternoon through a foot of snow. Leaving sixteen of them to spend the night at a roadhouse a few miles from the ferry on the Idaho side, Captain McConnell took three men with him to another ferry several miles down the river where they crossed over to the Oregon side and rode back up the river to the Washoe Ferry. Here they dismounted and three of them stayed at a distance, stamping their feet to keep warm. The fourth man, who was unknown at the ferry, went to the house and hammered on the door, shouting "Hello the house!" When a man answered, he called out that there was a party that must get across the river to Idaho, and because there was flowing ice, they would pay double the usual fee. One of the brothers lit a candle and opened the door a crack.

"Do you know him, Bill?" said the other brother.

"Never saw him before."

"Well, let him in."

Six men were sleeping in the house, guns hanging within reach. When the door was unchained, the vigilante, saying he was freezing to death, headed for the fireplace at the other end of the room. He gathered up an armful of dry sagebrush from a pile in the corner and threw it on the bed of coals. Fire flashed up the chimney. That was the signal to the three vigilantes outside, and in an instant the door was filled with revolvers. The wakening men didn't have a chance to reach their guns.

At sunup the rest of the vigilantes arrived, according to plan, and court went into session. Two of the captives turned out to be innocent Oregonians looking for a ranch, and they were sent on their way. One man was acquitted, one was given the regulation 24 hours to clear out, and the brothers who operated the ferry were sentenced to be hanged. After more discussion, this was decided to be more drastic than necessary, and the brothers also were allowed to leave the country.

Now the outlaws in the area really did become alarmed. The vigilantes were getting to be a downright nuisance. If a few of the leaders could be wiped out, especially the resourceful Captain McConnell, the Committee would probably fall apart. They went to Sheriff Opdyke for assistance. After spreading the word all through the communities that the vigilantes were just a bunch of cutthroats standing in the way of law and order, the sheriff had warrants issued for all the Payette Valley residents suspected of belonging to the Committee. He swore in a large number of deputies to serve the warrants, with Picket Corral men assigned the special job of riding up to Jerusalem Valley late at night to arrest the captain and take care he didn't reach Boise alive.

The rumor got around. A friend borrowed a good horse from the Boise Barracks and started the 18 miles of unbroken snow over the hills to warn the captain. A winter's night journey in that rough country was dangerous, but he arrived without accident, with his message.

The captain said it would be a pity to make such a distinguished party of deputies ride so far in bad weather to serve the papers; he would just ride down and meet them part way. A party of four started off down along the Payette River, expecting to meet the deputation around every bend.

But a hitch had occurred in the original plan of the deputies. They had decided to stop at a stage station until all the arrests had been made in the lower valley. As the four Jerusalem Valley men approached the station, they saw the row of guns propped against the outside of the building. There were no windows on that side and the Picket Corral men had no advance warning of their approach. They arrived at the station before someone happened to open the door and look out. He shouted and grabbed for a gun. A sharp command to "Drop it!" changed his mind and the door was jerked shut again. The horsemen grinned and proceeded on their way to Boise City. The Picket Corral deputies were so mortified at their failure to carry out their special assignment, they went across the river to a friend's ranch and drowned their humiliation in a big drunk.

The prisoners already in custody in Boise City were promptly sent home again, since the sheriff had no evidence they had violated any law. This was the last organized activity of the Payette Vigilance Committee. Also it might interest you to know that this enterprising sheriff eventually "resigned his position for cause," as Mr. McConnell notes in his "Early History of Idaho," and was later hanged in the Montana country. Mr. McConnell does not seem to have shed any tears.

Considering that these were some of the multitudinous occupations it took to keep William McConnell busy when he was 25, (and he lived to be 86), we are not surprised to learn he would still find time to become U.S. Deputy Marshal, cattleman, merchant, delegate to National Republican Convention, President of Oregon State Senate, member of Idaho Constitutional Convention, Idaho's first U.S. Senator after statehood, Governor of Idaho for two terms, Indian inspector, immigration inspector, and historian. Neither does it surprise us to read the words of his secretary when McConnell was governor. "There are no dull moments," noted J. J. Curtis, "in the executive offices."

Hill Beachy, the man who forced legal justice in Idaho.

Chapter 13

LEGAL JUSTICE COMES TO IDAHO

T HE MOST cold-blooded lot of murders in Idaho history was committed on a mountain trail between Bannack, Montana and Lewiston, Idaho, in October, 1863.

Lloyd Magruder was a well-known packer in North Idaho, who for two years made a living packing supplies into mining camps to sell. His final trip started in August with a pack train of goods bound for the mining camps at Bannack and Virginia City, Montana. Before starting, he stopped in at the Luna Hotel to say goodbye to the owner, Hill Beachy, who was an old friend.

Hill Beachy was a man who sometimes had premonitions, and he had one now. He had had a dream about the murder of this friend. It was so vivid that he had told his wife about it and they discussed it, and talked about telling Magruder about it. But Magruder had never had any trouble on his pack trips, and he would be sure to think they were crazy. They didn't say anything to him about the dream, but Beachy warned his friend of the dangers of toughs who hung about the camps and were on the trails, and he insisted on lending him a good gun to take along.

Even in those days of mule power, sixty animals loaded with supplies was a large train and very valuable. People stood on the main street of Lewiston to watch them go by, mule after mule. Among the watchers were three strangers: a man named Lowry, a man named Howard, and a man named Romain. They watched the mules file by, and they figured together. To camp each night near water and grass, and to load and unload big packs from sixty mules every day, the train might make 12 to 15 miles a day on the rough trails of the Bitterroot Mountains. It was 300 miles from Lewiston to Virginia City. It would take at least three weeks.

The strangers made their preparations and waited ten days, then started out. With few in number and lightly loaded, they could travel twice as fast as the train. Before the mining camps were reached, they overtook the train. They offered to help with the mules and the packs, just for their food, and as Magruder was really short-handed, and they seemed a jolly bunch of mountain men, they all finished the trip together.

In Virginia City, Magruder put up a big tent and set out his goods to sell. The strangers hung around, helping with the mules and watching with great interest the selling of the goods and the accumulation of gold dust. By the middle of October everything was sold and Magruder had about $30,000 in gold dust. He was anxious to get back to Lewiston to his family before an early snow would close the mountain passes, and he told the three men and a mountain trapper named William Page, and a couple of other men, that he would pay them well if they would ride along and help on the return trip. Two young brothers who had accumulated about $2000 in gold dust, and wanted to go home to Missouri, also joined the train. There were nine men altogether.

The outlaws had their plan ready and watched for a good place on the trail. One night when a snowstorm was threatening and they were camped near the edge of a cliff that stood several hundred feet above a gorge, they decided the time and place were right. They informed Page, the mountain trapper, that they were going to kill all the others, but they would let him live to act as their guide, and would give him a share of the gold dust; but if he didn't keep his mouth shut, they would kill him too.

Magruder was on night watch over the mule herd. Lowry came up behind him and killed him with an axe. The others were sleeping around the campfire, and were killed while they slept. All the murdered men were tied up in their blankets and thrown over the cliff. When daylight came, the outlaws selected five of the best mules to ride and pack, then drove the rest of the train into a canyon and killed them. They took what provisions they needed and burned the rest, loaded up the gold dust and started on their way.

They intended to bypass Lewiston, but there was ice flowing in the Clearwater River, so they slipped into town after dark, found a ranchman who would keep the mules, and under assumed names, took the early morning stage for Walla Walla.

Hill Beachy, Magruder's friend, heard about the three strangers and became suspicious. A few days later another party arrived from Bannack and he questioned them. They reported that Magruder's train had left Bannack before they did, and that eight men were traveling with him. Beachy hunted around and located the five mules left with the rancher. He recognized Magruder's saddle mule and his saddle right away.

Friendship in those rough days was the most valuable thing a man could possess, and it was taken very seriously. Hill Beachy was not only a loyal friend, he was a most unusual citizen. He went to the Governor of the Idaho Territory, Governor William Wallace, and obtained requests on the Governors of Oregon, Washington and California, for extradition of the murderers wherever they might be found. Armed with these, and taking along one man, Tom Pike, he drove to Walla Walla, rode the stage to Wallula, and took the steamer to Portland. He picked up information that the fugitives had been there a few days before, gambling and spending gold dust freely, but that they had now departed for San Francisco by steamship.

Beachy felt he couldn't afford to wait for the next steamer. Leaving Tom Pike to come on by boat, he started overland by stagecoach. The road to Sacramento was pure punishment, deep mud and chuckholes all the way. The stage traveled the clock around, only stopping to change horses and eat. After three days and nights cooped up in the Concord coach, they reached Yreka, California. There was a telegraph station at Yreka, and Beachy wired to the chief of police of San Francisco an account of the murders and a description of the fugitives. He asked that they be arrested and held for his arrival. The police department evidently had good men, for when Beachy arrived a few days later, he found the prisoners behind bars. Their gold dust was traced to the U.S. Mint. William Page, the trapper, made a full confession and gave an eye-witness account of the murders.

The handcuffed prisoners were turned over to Beachy on the authority of the papers he carried. He and Tom Pike started north with them, by steamer to Portland and Wallula, by stage to Lewiston.

They were met by a crowd of citizens carrying ropes, ready to deal out camp justice. Hill Beachy said no, he had given his word in San Francisco that the prisoners should have a fair trial by jury. They were his responsibility.

This was a lot more of a promise than you might think today. When the Territory of Idaho had been created the spring before, no laws had been provided under which to operate. The general laws of the United States were not adequate for criminal and civilian trials. The district court was scheduled to open its first term on January 5, without any code to make its actions legal.

On December 7, the day Beachy arrived with his prisoners, the first legislative assembly of the Idaho Territory got busy and met in its first session. Legislative action must have been much swifter in those days, for they promptly organized themselves and agreed to adopt the code of the Common Law of England for Idaho. It was signed on January 4, and the next day Judge Samuel Parks opened the first term of district court held in Idaho, and the trial of the murderers began.

William Page, because of turning State's evidence, went free. The three murderers, defended by an attorney, tried before a jury, were convicted of murder in the first degree, and were legally hanged on March 4, 1864.

Hill Beachy did not rest until the Mint at San Francisco released to the Magruder family the $17,000 the criminals had deposited.

And our Legislature, "for the great service Mr. Beachy has rendered the cause of law and order," appropriated $6244 for the heavy expenses of his pursuit and capture of the murderers.

Chapter 14

A PERIPATETIC CAPITAL

W HEN WE LOOK at the immense capitol building standing so solidly in the center of Boise, it certainly seems that Boise must always have been Idaho's capital. But that isn't so.

The discovery of gold in Orofino Creek brought a stampede of men from Walla Walla to Lewiston. So many men, in fact, that Congress cut a chunk out of Washington Territory and called it Idaho Territory. In 1863, President Lincoln named William Wallace first Governor of the Territory, and instructed him to choose a capital and hold a meeting of legislators there.

The Governor chose Lewiston. It wasn't much of a town yet, but a boomtown near goldfields grows like a mushroom. A year before, it had only six wooden buildings, and some tents. Now it had 40 log buildings and 120 tent buildings. There certainly were no churches, but there were three hotels, two livery stables, fifteen stores, a brewery, and saloons without number. There was a doctor, an assayer of gold, two lawyers, a blacksmith, a butcher, a baker, a dairyman, and a barber. No minister yet. Lewiston was a very tough town. The Portland Oregonian commented that in Lewiston, if you had a mule you didn't want stolen, "you must take him to bed with you."

But Lewiston was the gateway to the northern goldfields. Boats carried freight up the Columbia and Snake Rivers, and back down to The Dalles. A stage left Lewiston for the west every morning, and one started south every other day. Lewiston had a good headstart on the Boise Basin in the south, where a goldrush was just beginning. Boise City had not even been surveyed yet.

However, legislators from southern Idaho objected right away to having the capital at Lewiston. They said the population in the south would be larger than in the north, in no time. They said Lewiston was too far away. They said mountains and canyons cut it off from the rest of the Territory.

They were right about the population. When the goldrush really got going in the south, Boise Basin cast twenty times more votes than Lewiston did. Then Congress took a chunk out of Idaho Territory to form Montana Territory, and North Idaho was left with just a narrow panhandle, and many fewer people than before.

Drawing of Lewiston building where Idaho's first Territorial Legislature met.

Courtesy Idaho Historical Society

As soon as they were the majority, the legislators from the south passed a bill to move the capital to Boise City. A great howl went up from the north. They ran to the Court to get an injunction.

By now Idaho Territory had a new Governor, Caleb Lyon, an odd gentleman who always signed his name, "Caleb Lyon of Lyonsdale." (Appointees from the East didn't cotton to Idaho. In the first eight years of Idaho Territory, we had eight President-appointed Governors.) When Governor Lyon was packing up to move the capital to Boise, he heard by the grapevine that he was going to be arrested and prevented from leaving Lewiston. Quickly changing his arrangements, he hurried across the river into Washington Territory, leaving word he was going on "a hunting trip."

Idaho State Capitol building, Boise. Started 1905, completed 1920, cost $2,290,000.

Courtesy Idaho Dept. Tourism and Industrial Development

Frustrated in their intentions, the police served the papers on the Territorial Secretary, and kept a close watch on the Idaho Seal, the copy of the Laws, and other official records. Without these symbols of office, there couldn't be a capital somewhere else.

The fight went on in the courts and in the newspapers, and on the streets. There were black eyes and bloody noses all over the place.

At last President Lincoln sent out a new Territorial Secretary to see what he could do about straightening out the mess. Governor Lyon was still absent on his hunting trip, so Secretary C. DeWitt Smith became Acting Governor, with authority to take whatever action he found necessary.

Once again the northerners rushed to the Court to prevent the move. But Secretary Smith was evidently a man of more than ordinary courage and firmness. He did not go on a hunting trip. He sent for a guard of soldiers from nearby Fort Lapwai. He obtained the Idaho Seal, the Laws, and the other official records that were needed, and the guard convoyed him to Boise City. The party arrived there safely on April 14, 1865 (which, although they did not know it until later, was the day President Lincoln was assassinated).

That ended the capital's travels, but for many years afterward (and perhaps even now in Lewiston), you could hear people scream, "Boise City stole our capital!"

Chapter 15

CHARLES OSTNER
AND HIS STATUE

THE NEXT time you are exploring the first floor of Idaho's capitol building and see the gold-leafed statue of General George Washington on his prancing horse, stop a minute and think about the man who carved them.

Charles Leopold Ostner was born in Germany in 1828, and studied art in Heidelberg. He got into trouble in a revolt of young men against the German monarchy, and when he was 18 he went off to America in a hurry. Traveling around the new country, he fell in love with its space and freedom. He lived for awhile in the German colony in San Francisco, and married one of the young women there. He prospected the canyons of California, but there the gold was running out, and presently he joined the gold rush to northern Idaho. No luck there, either, and when gold was discovered in the Boise Basin, he was ready to move south.

He and another man loaded their picks and shovels and gold-pans on a burro with food for the trip, and started down the winding mountain trail that Packer John Welch had blazed between the mining camps of the north and the south.

The other man wasn't a very pleasant fellow, and he was in a bad mood. Plodding along the rough trail, he brooded over his troubles. He was sick of looking for gold. If he could somehow get back to San Francisco, things would go better for him. The stubborn Ostner would never agree to a change of plans, he knew, so he kept his mouth shut and watched for his chance. It came somewhere along the trail where the timber grew thick. Quietly he sneaked out of sight with the burro and all the supplies; and eventually he made his way out to civilization.

When Ostner missed him, of course he turned back to look for him. Not that he imagined he had been deserted on purpose. Men in western wilds didn't treat one another like that. He simply thought his partner had taken a wrong turn somewhere, and he must find him.

Charles Ostner evidently didn't have a very good sense of direction. He had no food in his pockets and he wasn't trained to live off the land. The poor man wandered for forty days, completely lost, back and forth across steep ridges, and in and out of deep canyons. At last Packer John ran across him accidently, all skin and bones

General Washington statue carved by Charles L. Ostner, 1865-69.

and out of his head, above Garden Valley. He managed to get him to a cabin where he fed him and nursed him back to partial health; but Charles Ostner was never very strong again.

You would think that this terrible experience would have given him enough of Idaho. But no. Idaho he loved, Idaho was where he wanted to spend the rest of his life. Prospecting had brought him no luck, so now he bought a piece of land, with a toll-bridge attached. The bridge was just wide enough for a pack train to cross the river, and whoever crossed it paid a toll to the owner. The property was also an overnight stopping and eating place for men on the trail between Placerville and the mining camps in North Idaho. This would be a profitable business during the gold rush years. Ostner sent for his wife and children to come from San Francisco. They traveled up the coast to Portland, and on up the Columbia River to Wallula by steamboat, then by dead axle wagon, and finally by pack train to Placerville, making the Ostners the first family in Garden Valley.

All this time, even when traveling and hunting gold, Charles Ostner was always drawing or painting or carving. He liked to do horses and scouts and miners and Indians and wild animals. And now he had a dream of using his talent to make something for Idaho, something that would express his feeling for the freedom of his adopted land.

To him, George Washington, as General-in-Chief of the American army fighting the tyranny of England, was the symbol of American freedom. One winter, snowed-in in a North Idaho mining camp Ostner had made a statue of General Washington out of ice and snow, just as they make ice statues now for the winter carnival in McCall. Now he decided he would carve such a statue out of wood, exactly like the one he had made of ice, and give it to Idaho in memory of her early pioneers.

He selected a Ponderosa pine and hauled it by hand-cart over the snow to his home by the toll-bridge, and went to work. He didn't have any real carving tools; he had only carpenter's saws and chisels. During the daytime he worked on his farm and at the toll-bridge, so the carving had to be done at night. His children took turns holding a torch of pitch-pine to give him light to work by. The carving took him four years. He copied the face of General Washington from the picture on a postage stamp.

He wrote to the Territorial Government in Boise about his project, but the officers there took it as a kind of joke. The idea of a farmer somewhere up on the Payette River carving a statue of General Washington mounted on a horse, struck them as comical.

He finished the statue and painted it bronze. It was the middle of winter and the snow was deep, but he couldn't wait on weather. The Legislature was to meet in Boise in January and he was eager to present his gift. He loaded it into a wagon, covered it over with blankets, and started on his way. At each mining camp he would stop, collect a small fee from the miners, and remove the blankets. You can imagine that in mid-December, in a snowed-in mining camp, the statue made quite a sensation!

There is a story that some legislators riding horseback down from the North on their way to Boise, overtook the wagon covered over with blankets, and had the sudden idea there had been an Indian massacre and the bodies were being brought out. When Ostner pulled away the blankets and revealed a statue of General Washington, the legislators' eyes nearly popped out of their heads.

Whether that really happened or is just a good story, the Territorial officers in Boise certainly stopped laughing about a farmer carving a statue when they saw it. It was presented to the State of Idaho in a public ceremony, in a heavy snowstorm on January 6, 1869. The Legislature was so impressed, it voted a gift of $2500 to Charles Ostner for his devoted work, and the statue was placed on the capitol grounds.

In 65 years the weather did a good deal of damage, and in 1934 it was repaired and covered with gold leaf and moved inside the capitol building.

Then it developed that ignorant vandals with no feeling for the love and work that had gone into the carving, were more damaging than weather had been. Somebody broke the spurs off General Washington's boots. Somebody twisted the sword scabbard in two. Somebody tore the martingale off the horse's neck.

In 1966, the statue was restored once more and covered with another coat of gold leaf at a cost of $3,000, and it was enclosed in a protective glass case. And that is the way you will see it now.

Chapter 16

THE DISCOVERY OF
THE BUNKER HILL ORE

Noah Kellogg hunted silver
In Eighty-Five or -Six
With a pious-looking burro
That was Satan-full of tricks
Such as scraping under branches,
Dislocating grub and picks.
Hee haw.

This burro had a toothy smile
That hid a toothy plot.
Long lashes drooping over eyes
Concealed their wicked thought.
When Noah chanced to turn his back
He wished that he had not!
Hee haw!

Poor Noah was a hard-luck man,
He searched the hills in vain.
His toes poked through his tattered boots,
His spare ribs pokcd out plain.
Gaunt gizzard is poor company
In mud and wind and rain.
Hee haw.

Beat at last, was Noah Kellogg.
Down, in Milo Gulch he lay
To forget his sorry troubles
And await the Judgment Day—
But that little joker raised him
With a galvanizing bray:
HEE HAW! HEE HAW!

Noah resurrected, and he
Shot up with a cry,
"No rabbit-eared canary
Mocks *me* the day I die!"
The burro grinned and frolicked off
As Noah's club let fly.

Thump to the rump! The answering kick
Shattered a ridge of rock—
And *there* was the gleam! the long-sought gleam!
Noah near died of shock.
The richest store of silver-lead
The whole world had in stock!
Hee haw!

A pious-looking burro.

Photo by Duane Garrett

Chapter 17

THE CIVIL WAR AND IDAHO

IDAHO WAS barely born when the Civil War broke out. They were so far apart, you might not think they would matter to one another, but in a democracy, any large happening affects everybody.

Idaho's earliest years saw its greatest mining of gold. Shipped to the San Francisco Mint, our gold bars helped pay the Union soldiers and other expenses of a Government impoverished by the collapse of normal business. So Idaho had a hand in preserving the Union.

On our side of the picture, the Civil War caused hundreds of refugees from ruined Missouri to strike out for the mines of Idaho. On the map of Idaho you can find the names Atlanta, Dixie, Leesburg, Secession Ridge. And if it seems to you that some fanatics are still fighting the Civil War over a hundred years later, you should have been around the mining camps in the 1860s! An argument could easily blow up into a battle, and end in bloodshed.

In pioneer communities, men didn't interest themselves too much in politics, but in Idaho the Democratic party chanced to be a bit in the majority. This made it a magnet to lawless men, whose policy it was to join whichever party was strongest, so they could influence legislation to their own interest. Missourians were Democrats because their fathers and their grandfathers had been, and when they came to Idaho, of course they lined up with the Democrats, so that now they had a solid majority in the legislature.

The Republican Congress, which provided our Territorial Governors and Secretaries, and some of our laws, was determined to keep Southerners in their place. It passed a bill requiring any public official in the Territory of Idaho including legislators to take an oath of loyalty to the United States. Naturally, our Missourian Confederate sympathizers refused to do so. Whereupon, in 1867, the Territorial Secretary refused to pay them for their services.

The infuriated members organized a rough-house and threw the legislative furniture out of the windows. Territorial Governor David Ballard promptly sent over to the Boise Fort for troops to restore order. Within an hour they arrived and stood at rest in front of the legislative building.

Within another half-hour the legislative members, whether Confederate in sympathy or not, signed the oath and received their pay. Sometimes our strongest convictions are persuaded by our pocketbooks.

"Out the Window!"

Drawing by Virginia Hibbs

Chapter 18

HOW MUCH IS IT WORTH?

WHEN OUR MINES were producing richly, we wanted Congress to give Idaho a mint. Freight and insurance on ore sent to the San Francisco mint were expensive, taking five to ten cents of the miner's dollar. Some local gold buyers did pay fair prices, but many were cheats, and speculators charged large discounts for the convenience.

Idaho officials worked on Congress for four years without result. We then lowered our sights and asked for an assay office and this went over better. In 1869, Congress voted $75,000 to build Idaho an assay office.

Alexander Rossi had a farm at the edge of Boise City, and he donated one square block for the building. It was a block of uncleared desert sagebrush, and people objected that it was "rather far from the business district." You can see the block now, bounded by Main and Idaho, Second and Third Streets. Mr. Rossi's farmhouse was across the street, where Boise's tallest apartment building now stands.

Construction was interrupted, but the building was completed in 1871. A large, square, dignified building in the exact center of its block. The walls were two feet thick, of sandstone from the Table Rock quarry. Heavy iron bars on the windows and doors gave newcomers the idea that it was the jail.

It was the pride of Idaho. Citizens donated trees and shrubs, and what is more, they brought a shovel and planted them. Living quarters for the chief assayer's family were on the second floor. The guards lived in the basement. On the first floor were the assaying and melting rooms, with furnaces, the laboratory, vaults, storage cabinets and offices.

For a number of years they were very busy. Prospectors brought samples of ore to find out how good a strike they had made. Bullion arrived in the form of bars of alloy from placer and dredging operations. Individual miners brought nuggets and gold dust in pokes. A citizen could even bring jewelry or gold fillings from teeth and get them assayed, which was popular during the 1930s when the depression was on.

In the early years, the main business was determining the amount of pure gold and silver in bullion that was to go to the mint.

Idaho Assay office, 1971.

Courtesy Idaho Historical Society

The assayer melted down selected samples, removed any foreign matter, and poured the remaining metal into molds to form bars. These were assayed to find the proportions of gold, silver, and base metal, and the depositor was paid for the assayed value. When a good deal of the purchased bullion had accumulated in the vaults, the assayer melted it into mint bars and shipped it to one of the United States mints to be made into coins.

Gradually the mining business ran out. In 1933, the Assay Office closed. The U. S. Forest Service used it for offices for nearly forty years. Now that the Forest Service has a building of its own, the United States has deeded the building to the State of Idaho. Most appropriately, it is to become the Idaho Historical Society's mining museum.

Chapter 19

SHE WINS THE VOTE

W E THINK OF Idaho as conservative. Her citizens aren't in a hurry to take up newfangled ideas. Then isn't it surprising that our state was among the first four to allow women to vote (which certainly *was* a newfangled idea)? The other three were Rocky Mountain states too—Wyoming, Utah and Colorado. It must be something about the high, free air.

Voting wasn't mentioned in the U.S. Constitution. The delegates couldn't agree about voting rights, so they finally left them out altogether, to be decided by some future amendment. And since women never had voted, they continued not to vote.

After awhile, early seeds of women's lib must have begun to sprout, for women started working to get an amendment added to the Constitution that would give them the right to vote. When the Civil War ended, the Republicans pushed the Fifteenth Amendment through Congress, to give the vote to negro men. Women's rights' leaders were infuriated because the amendment did not include women. They had to fight fifty years longer before they succeeded, in 1920, with the Nineteenth Amendment.

"Meanwhile, back at the ranch," as they used to say in the silent movies, women went on working at the state level to persuade their legislatures to amend state constitutions to give them the vote. In Idaho the battle started very early, in 1871, and surprisingly, it wasn't a woman who started it, it was a man.

The bill was put to the Idaho legislature by a young Welsh doctor from Malad City, William Morgan. We don't know why he felt strongly about this particular matter; perhaps his young English wife urged him on.

It stirred up a lot of argument. Some gentlemen tried to flatter women out of the idea, declaring that ladies were too delicate and refined to mix in rough-house politics. A Boise editor named McGonigle, like many men before him, took it upon himself to interpret God's intentions concerning women, stating that He didn't intend them to be mixed up in "horse racing, prize fighting, or voting for sheriff." The final vote tied, 11 to 11, and the bill was lost for 25 years.

Abigail Scott Duniway — one reason women can vote.

Courtesy Idaho Historical Society

But the possibility of getting the vote, having been planted in the minds of Idaho women, began to grow there. Copies of a women's rights newspaper, published in Portland, found their way into Idaho homes. Its publisher, Abigail Duniway, had two sons ranching in the Lost River country, and when she visited them, she would make speeches around the state. She was a fine, lively speaker, and several times the Idaho legislature invited her to speak to them.

About this time, the Women's Christian Temperance Union, which was fighting the use of whisky all over the nation, began to organize little unions in Idaho towns. They invited the women's-vote people to join with them and combine their goals, but the women's-voters were afraid the W.C.T.U. would do their cause more harm than good. Back in the East, Carrie Nation was chopping up saloons with her little hatchet, enraging men by the thousands. The women's-voters didn't want to enrage men; they wanted to charm them into voting their way. If women could only win the vote, they reasoned, then they would have the power to bring about other improvements.

It was 1895 before Idaho women organized their own Suffrage Association. They didn't add up to a thousand members, but there were little clubs sprouting up all over the state. Carrie Chapman Catt and other officers of the national association came out to Idaho to help with the campaign. With important help from William Balderston, editor of the Idaho Statesman, they won the backing of all four political parties that were then represented in the legislature —Republican, Democratic, Populist, and Silver Republican. In 1896, the amendment passed, two to one.

Immediately women went to work to change things that had been aggravating them for years—to make gambling illegal, to close saloons on Sunday, to prohibit child labor, to protect girls until age 18, to give married women rights over their own property, to support libraries, and to put a domestic science course in the university.

An editorial summed up the business in 1906: "The political machine and crooked politics stand in constant fear of the women's vote. When women act, they act for better morals and politics, but they dread to take hold. They are like sheep crossing a stream. They must be pushed in, but once in, there is no turning back until the opposite bank is reached."

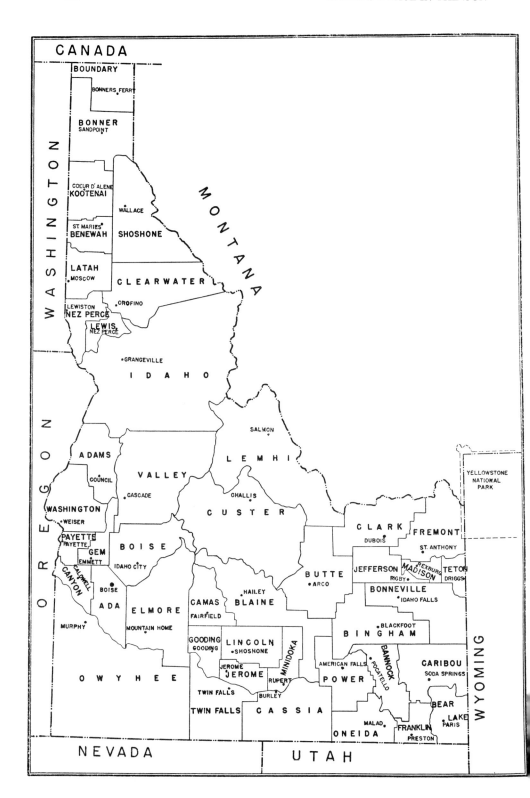

Chapter 20

THE IDAHO COUNTIES
IN SIXTY SECONDS

Gem State students, would you like to know
The Forty-four counties in Idaho?

Check your watch:

Ada is the first, with our capital town.
Adams' Seven Devils go straight up and down.
Then ten counties that start with "B":
Bannock and *Bear Lake* and *Benewah*—three—
Bingham, Blaine, Boise, Bonner, and then
Bonneville, Boundary, Butte make ten.
All the next seven begin with "C":
Camas and *Canyon* and *Caribou*—three—
Cassia, Clark, Clearwater, finally *Custer,*
Are the Idaho "C's" that we can muster.
Elmore, Franklin, Fremont, Gem,
Gooding and *Idaho,* don't forget them.
Flat lands of *Jefferson,* potatoes of *Jerome,*
Kootenai and *Latah* (We're on the stretch home!)
Lemhi and *Lewis* (Hurry, hurry, hurry!)
Lincoln with its ice caves, very, very br-r-ry!
*Madison—Minidoka—*then *Nez Perce—*
(Our Indian accent grows worse and worse.)
Oneida and *Owyhee* (A little faster, please.)
Payette and *Power* are the only "P's".
Shoshone, Teton, Twin Falls—(Almost done)—
Valley County and *Washington!*

We made it.

Young Chief Joseph.

Chapter 21

THE DISPOSSESSED

THE MOST FAMOUS of all Idahoans is Young Chief Joseph. The most famous words of our history are his vow, "From where the sun now stands, I will fight no more forever."

We believe Indians have lived in the Idaho area at least 10,000 years, but we know next to nothing about them before 1805, when Lewis and Clark came through. When the explorers came over the Continental Divide down into the Lemhi Valley, they met the helpful Shoshonis, who supplied them with horses to continue their journey west. They met the Nez Perce on the Clearwater River, and when they returned on their way home eastward, they camped with them for six weeks while waiting for the snow to melt in the mountain passes.

Before white men broke in on them, Indians lived a free, simple, outdoor life. Their problems were food, weather, and battling other tribes for hunting grounds. After horses arrived on the Snake River Plains in the 1700s, they could ride over the Bitterroot mountains to hunt buffalo, and they could battle for hunting grounds farther from home. Salmon in the central and northern rivers was a main item of food. They ate it fresh in summer, and dried it for winter. A few Idaho prairies were as blue as lakes when the camas lily bloomed. They dug the bulbs, baked them, and ground them up into a kind of flour. In some areas there were deer, elk, antelope, bighorn sheep, bear, rabbits and squirrels. In good years there were huckleberries. But there was never quite enough food for everybody all the year round. Most of their time they spent hunting for food and preserving it.

When the fur traders came, the Indians learned the value of fur pelts to trade for the goods of the whites. Unfortunately, their favorite goods were guns and whisky.

Idaho Indians were fortunate in their missionaries. The Reverend Spalding with the Nez Perce at the Lapwai Mission, and the Jesuits with the Coeur d'Alenes at the Cataldo Mission, were truly dedicated to the best interests of the Indians. It was because these men were truly Christian, that our northern Indians remained friendly to whites long after one would have expected them to turn hostile.

For we treated them shamefully. We guaranteed certain lands to their use, but when white people wanted these lands, we took them back. Where gold was found, miners took over the land; where there was rich soil, ranchers settled on it. Indian lands shrank and shrank, until at last they were penned on reservations sometimes with poor soil and not much wild game. They, who had had the whole continent to rove over, now must ask the newcomer white men's permission to step outside the boundaries of the reservation. Wealthy sportsmen, who killed not for food but for the sport of it, came every year from the East to hunt on ground forbidden to Indians.

It isn't surprising Indians finally went on the rampage. What is surprising is that they didn't do it sooner. They held back until emigrant wagons were coming by the hundreds, and white families were building their houses and barns on the best land. But once they understood it was the final intention of the whites to take all the best and ram the leavings down the Indians' throats, the Indian attitude violently changed. They became cruel and merciless, they would commit any atrocity to strike terror in the hearts of these white thieves. We think with horror of the massacres of settlers and wagon trains, but if it had been ourselves committing these crimes, we would have called it "protecting our people."

It didn't do them any good in the long run, of course. There wasn't room for both whites and Indians, and we had them inevitably outnumbered. They were doomed. But before they finally gave up, those first Idahoans gave us latecomers three good runs for our money.

The first was the Nez Perce War in 1877. For twenty years the various Governors of the Territory had been trying to restrict the Nez Perce to certain areas. The tribes of Upper Nez Perce didn't kick up too much fuss. They signed a treaty and accepted blankets in payment. It was another story with the Lower Nez Perce. Chief Whitebird had a wandering tribe that fished and hunted along the Salmon River. Old Joseph's tribe lived in the lovely Wallowa Valley in well-built lodges, raising cattle and fine horses. They would have nothing to do with a treaty. Old Joseph told Washington Territorial Governor Isaac Stevens that no man owned any part of the earth, and he couldn't sell or trade what he didn't own.

Things drifted along a few years while more whites came to settle and to demand more of the best land. Old Joseph, steadfastly refusing to sign a treaty, warned his people never to accept any present from the whites, not so much as a single blanket. "After awhile they will claim you have accepted payment for your country," said the shrewd old chief.

The whites never gave up. In 1863, they presented another treaty for signing, and this one claimed the Wallowa Valley. The upper Nez Perce, whose lands would be part of the Lapwai reservation and who would therefore not be uprooted, reluctantly signed the treaty. The white men claimed this as authorization from the majority, and ordered the Wallowa Nez Perce to leave their valley and move to the reservation at Fort Lapwai.

Rule by vote of a majority had never been an Indian principle. If a majority of a tribe agreed on something, it didn't bind those who disagreed; they could go off and live as they liked. Old Joseph was so angry at the majority ruling and the order to leave the Wallowa Valley, he tore up a Bible a missionary had given him, and which he had prized. He set up poles to mark a boundary where his people lived.

Soon afterward he died, and Young Joseph became chief of the Wallowa tribe. Young Joseph petitioned President Grant to let his people stay in the valley where they had been born and where their parents were buried. The president finally agreed; he withdrew the Wallowa Valley from settlement by white people.

But the Wallowa Valley was a long way from President Grant's authority. White settlers crowded in around the edge of the valley, and when they could, they stole Indian cattle. Gold miners in nearby mountains stole their horses.

In two years of steady pressure from the white men, President Grant took back his promise, and gave the Wallowa Indians thirty days to move onto the Lapwai reservation. Angry young warriors, with the sympathy of Chief Whitebird, wanted to go on the warpath. But there were fewer than 100 warriors, and there were three companies of soldiers stationed at Fort Lapwai under Civil War General ("One-Armed Soldier") Howard. Chief Joseph knew his people wouldn't have a chance. He counseled them to go peaceably to the reservation.

They gathered together what possessions they could take, and started. The Snake River was running high with melting snows, and was dangerous to cross, but they got the women and children safely over on buffalo hide rafts. While they were busy at this, some white men stole some of the cattle waiting to cross. That did it for the young warriors. Still Joseph counseled peace as the only way. They called him a coward. He stood fast.

A few of the hot-headed young men did not give in. They slipped away into the Whitebird and Salmon River canyons and horribly butchered, looted and burned out eleven white people. That put an end to a peaceable settlement.

Joseph decided that if they could get across the Bitterroot Mountains, there was a chance they might be left alone to live among their friends, the Crow Indians. Camping at Whitebird Creek, they began to collect their livestock.

There wasn't enough time to carry out that plan. General Howard, at word of the outrages committed on settlers, ordered Colonel Perry and 100 cavalry, stationed at Cottonwood House on the prairie above Grangeville, to ride out and look over the situation. They didn't really expect much trouble in rounding up the Indians, who were burdened with families, livestock and possessions.

The Indians had the advantage of being familiar with the countryside. They hid themselves in the brush and gullies, and Joseph watched the approach of the horsemen over the hill through powerful binoculars. They let the soldiers get a glimpse of a few warriors, drawing them on into the rough ravine. Suddenly the Indians let loose with their guns from all directions. They were deadly shots, and the soldiers were out in the open. Thirty-four soldiers were killed at once, and the others, thrown into confusion and many of them unhorsed, were chased back up over Whitebird Hill and almost to Grangeville. The Indians came out of the skirmish with a fresh supply of carbines and ammunition.

General Howard decided to handle the situation himself. He brought heavy reinforcements to the Salmon River. He ran up an American flag over his camp, and across the river the Nez Perce derisively hung up a red blanket and invited the soldiers to come on over.

Some wise old hands rode out from Mount Idaho, the county seat, to give General Howard a piece of advice. They told him of a ford the Indians often used to cross the Salmon to get up onto the prairie. If the general would set a guard at that ferry, he could prevent their coming over. General Howard didn't take kindly to advice from civilians. He said he appreciated their helpfulness, but he was a trained soldier and he would conduct the war in his own way. The wise old hands rode back to Mount Idaho.

The next thing anybody knew, the Indians did indeed cross the Salmon at the ferry, and climbed out of the canyon up to the prairie. They set up camp a few miles from Cottonwood House, where Colonel Perry and what was left of his cavalry, had taken refuge. The colonel sent out a party of ten to scout the neighborhood. They ran into an ambush and not one was left alive. Much encouraged, the Indians laid siege to Cottonwood House.

Word got through somehow to Mount Idaho to send their volunteers. Captain Randall raised seventeen volunteers (who have come down in our history as the "Brave Seventeen"), and they headed their horses for Cottonwood. They ran into a large band of warriors in a bad lay of land, and tried to reach a knoll where they would be above the level of the Indians. On their side, the Indians tried to get the whites on the run, so they could pick them off, one by one. Captain Randall told his volunteers their only chance was to charge the Indians, whooping, hollering and shooting. Some of them were the finest shots in the country, and their unexpected attack took the Indians by surprise. They drew back to conduct the battle from a safer distance.

The soldiers inside Cottonwood House could see the desperate battle, and they begged Colonel Perry for permission to ride out to help. The colonel refused. The whites were hopelessly outnumbered and he believed they couldn't be saved. It would be suicidal to attempt their rescue. When the soldiers couldn't stand it any longer, they rode out without the colonel's permission (and the colonel afterward had their leader arrested for insubordination).

By now, other parties of citizen volunteers arrived from Dayton, Washington, and from Lewiston, and the Indians withdrew. Many of the "Brave Seventeen" were wounded, and three were killed, including Captain Randall.

The Indians decided they had delayed long enough; it was time to get out of the country. When they reached the Clearwater River, they found their friend, Chief Looking Glass, waiting for them with his band of warriors. They were using the time of waiting to plunder the local ranches, stirring up the situation a little more.

Volunteers from Mount Idaho arrived again, and finally General Howard got his heavily laden troops moving and marched in. The battle of the Clearwater took place a few miles from Kooskia. General Howard's army had twice the fighting men the Indians had, and they were better equipped with rifles and ammunition. They also had howitzers, with which they bombarded the Indians' camp and positions. It made it too hot for the Indians. After two days of heavy fighting, they took off for Kamiah and the Lolo Trail. They must get over the Bitterroots to the land of the Crows.

There were now 250 warriors, 450 old people, women and children, a lot of baggage, and 2,000 horses. Even so, they were well acquainted with the country, and they thought they could outdistance the army.

They might have been able to do it, if this had been the little private war with General Howard's men, that Chief Joseph thought it was. What Joseph didn't know, was that the Indians were going to have to fight practically the whole United States Army. Greatly embarrassed over the defeat at Whitebird Hill, General Howard was taking no more chances. After hurriedly drawing extra cavalry from Fort Walla Walla, and infantry from Fort Vancouver, he requested troops to be brought from Alaska, Fort Boise, and Camp Harney; and all available units from Oregon, Nevada and California. He also asked that General ("Atlanta to the Sea") Sherman send infantry from Atlanta, Georgia, and General ("Twenty Miles Away") Sheridan have cavalry ready in Montana to intercept the Nez Perce.

With these troops arrowing in on them from all directions, the Indians were in deep trouble. On the Lolo Trail they succeeded in bypassing a barricade the troops built in a narrow pass to block them, and they did make it over the mountains. But they did not find the help they had hoped for, when they reached Montana. The Crow Indians turned a cool shoulder on them, not wanting to get mixed up in the fracas. The Nez Perce would have to go it alone.

Believing they had outdistanced General Howard, the Nez Perce turned south toward hunting country they knew well. But they didn't know that Colonel Gibbon was marching from Fort Missoula. In a surprise dawn attack on the Indian tepees at Big Hole, the Nez Perce lost eighty people, more than half of them women and children. They inflicted heavy losses on the troops, too, but General Howard was arriving with reinforcements. ("Day after Tomorrow" Howard, was what Chief Joseph called him.) Laying a trap, the Indians captured most of the general's pack mules, leaving him crippled for transport of supplies and ammunition.

Then the Indians cut across the northwest corner of Yellowstone Park and headed for Canada, where Sitting Bull and his Sioux had escaped the year before, after annihilating General Custer's army. In a month of hard travel, they made it across the Missouri River and into the Bear's Paw Mountains. They may have believed they had reached Canada. At any rate, they were short of food and needed to get some buffalo. Chief Joseph was in charge of the women and children and old people, and they were in bad shape. He ordered a pause to rest the horses and hunt.

It was a fatal mistake. They had marched 1,300 miles, and now they lost their chance at freedom by forty miles. General ("Bear Coat") Miles was coming from eastern Montana with 600 cavalry, and thirty Sioux and Cheyenne scouts to cut across their path. In bitter fighting, Chief Looking Glass, one of the great campaign leaders of the Nez Perce, was killed.

Chief Joseph was treacherously made prisoner while under the U.S. Army flag of truce. He refused to talk terms while being held a prisoner. The Indians won his release by capturing a white officer and threatening his life.

Chief Whitebird and the deadly accurate fire of the Nez Perce held the troops off a few more days, in the midst of a freezing blizzard. Then General Howard arrived once more with reinforcements. Joseph realized that the dwindling Nez Perce army was doomed. After days of parley, he delivered his noble speech of surrender.

After dark, Chief Whitebird and a band of unyielding young warriors crept through the ravines in small groups and ran for the freedom of the Canadian border.

General Miles, an honorable man, tried for years to get the U.S. Government to make good his promise that Joseph and his people would be sent back to the reservation at Fort Lapwai, but he failed. They were shipped to Fort Leavenworth, Kansas, as prisoners of war. Nearly one hundred died on that swampy bottomland. The remainder were then taken to Oklahoma Territory, where many died of malaria. By 1885, only 287 were left alive. 136 of these were finally taken to the reservation at Fort Lapwai. Joseph, and what warriors were left, were sent to Nespelem on the Colville reservation (a few miles from where Grand Coulee now dams the Columbia River.) In 1904, Joseph died and was buried there. The doctor at the Indian Agency listed the cause of death "a broken heart."

There was no nobility on either side in our two other Indian wars.

The year after the Nez Perce war, the Bannocks, assigned to Fort Hall reservation, went as usual to Camas Prairie (where Fairfield is now) to set up their tepees and get busy with their annual harvest of the camas root. This area had been guaranteed to them in a treaty with the United States.

Imagine their fury when they found that white ranchers had turned their livestock onto the prairie, and droves of hogs were rooting out the camas. The Bannocks went berserk.

Led by Chief Buffalo Horn, they started west and south, murdering and burning as they went. They crossed the Snake River at Glenn's Ferry, and headed for Jordan Valley, where there were a lot of stock ranches. The terrified white settlers cleared out of their way, until the Indians reached the small mining community of South Mountain, 25 miles south of Silver City. There they were engaged is a desperate skirmish by thirty citizen volunteers from the Silver City mining camp. Chief Buffalo Horn was killed, which took the heart out of the Indian band.

However, they went on for a couple of months, murdering and plundering as far west as John Day Valley, Oregon. Through June and July they were pursued by citizen volunteers and soldiers, but they traveled so fast and so elusively, it was hard to force them to a decisive battle. Many were killed and wounded on both sides. Finally, to avoid capture or annihilation, the Bannocks scattered into small bands and melted away into the mountains. Gradually they made their way back to the protection of the reservation at Fort Hall.

Our third and last Indian War, the Sheepeater War of 1879, was a crazy business from start to finish. When it was finally over, it turned out there were only fifteen Indian warriors involved, but the trouble and embarrassment they caused the United States Army, couldn't have been more effectively accomplished by a thousand. Hundreds of soldiers marched 1,200 miles more than four months, pursuing the Indians up and down the cruelest terrain in the state. One soldier was killed, others were wounded, frostbitten, and laid low by mountain fever. They lost sixty horses and mules, with packloads of ammunition and food. It was a wonderful demonstration of the advantage to the side who knew the country.

The original Sheepeater Indians were a small group who had lived for generations in the rugged Salmon River mountains, their main item of food being the bighorn sheep. After the Bannock War in 1878, they were joined by other Indians to avoid being put on the Fort Hall reservation. In what is now the Idaho Primitive Area, among the wild Bighorn Crags, surely they would not be discovered by the whites.

In May, 1879, word reached the Indian Agent at Fort Lemhi that five Chinese miners had been murdered in February at the mining camp at Orogrande, presumably by Sheepeater Indians. The army was ordered to look into the matter as soon as they could get through the snow. Captain Reuben Bernard started with a troop of 62 cavalry-men from the Boise barracks, and Lieutenant Henry Catley with a detachment of mounted infantrymen from Camp Howard in north Idaho.

Bernard's men pushed through deep snow and flooding streams and finally reached Orogrande, having lost six mules and their pack loads in the first week. At Orogrande, they found the dead Chinese, still frozen after five months. One was frozen with his arms and legs sticking out at right angles to his body, and someone with a grue-some sense of humor, had set him on all fours, put an old packsaddle on him, and loaded it with picks and shovels. In later investigation, there seemed a good deal of doubt whether Indians had been involved at all. White miners seemed more likely. The outrage to the dead Chinese had rather the brand of brutal jokes practiced by frontier rowdies.

However, the soldiers had been ordered to round up the Sheep-eaters, so they started out on an old Indian trail down Loon Creek. Melting snows had turned the stream into a roaring river the mules could not ford. The rocky canyon was so hard on the animals' feet, the troop made their way up to the mountain ridge. This did not prove any better, for they floundered over fallen timber and deep snowdrifts, and several mules slipped over the cliffs. When some of the soldiers began coming down with mountain fever, the troop made its way back to Cape Horn to recover without ever having glimpsed an Indian.

In the meantime, Lieutenant Catley's troop had been blocked by snow from getting farther than Warren's Ranch near the South Fork of the Salmon river, and they stayed there more than a month. On July 17, they managed to cross the flooded South Fork and push into the mountains. Ten days later they had a glimpse of two Indian horses, their first sign of Indian presence. Catley was a little slow in acting on the information, and the Indians had plenty of time to get ready for the troop.

High up on the other side of Big Creek, the Indians built a rock fortification overlooking the narrow ledge along which in due time the soldiers came riding, single file. Two were immediately wounded, and equipment was lost. Catley hastily ordered a retreat (for which he was later court-martialed.) Next day when the soldiers attempted to climb the ridge to avoid the hazardous canyon trail, they were met by Indian fire from both above and below. They were convinced there were hundreds of the enemy.

The Indians captured pack animals lagging behind, that happened to be carrying most of the rations. The soldiers unloaded the rest of the mules and tried to take cover among the baggage on the high, bare ridge. The Indians set fire to brush and trees below, all around the mountain. Drafts of air brought the fire straight upward. The troop saved itself by madly digging a fire trench around the top of the ridge. For fourteen hours the Indians kept them prisoners there. Desperate with thirst, they broke open a keg of vinegar to drink. You will find the name on the map today, "Vinegar Hill." When darkness fell, the soldiers evacuated their inconvenient position, abandoning their property, and escaped to Warm Springs, twelve miles from Warren's Ranch where they had started.

Greatly cheered and encouraged by this easy success, the Sheep-eaters began to go farther afield to express their independence. They visited isolated ranches and took potshots at men putting up their hay.

In mid-August, Captain Bernard with enlarged forces started

again in pursuit, this time from Elk Creek. This time the troop was going to be cagey, it would attack the Indians from two directions. But somehow the supply trains never managed to keep up, and snows and rains started again. No matter how hard the soldiers tried to prevent it, the Indians always managed to hide above them, where they could shoot down. At the end of the month the exhausted men, dressed in rags and living on mule meat, returned to Boise.

In September, a final expedition started off, on Catley's original route from Warren's Ranch. This was a new company under a new commander, Lieutenant Farrow, and it was accompanied by twenty Umatilla scouts from Pendleton. It takes an Indian to catch an Indian. The scouts found the Sheepeaters' camps, one after another, and the soldiers kept them on the run. By October, the Indians were run ragged and began to come in and surrender, two or three at a time. In the end, only 51 Indians were found, including men, women and children and the original fifteen warriors. They were taken to live at the Fort Hall Agency.

But, if you are a mountain climber with a passion for clambering around that precipitous country, don't be altogether surprised someday if you run across a few Sheepeaters happily going about their business among the Bighorn Crags. How do we know we rounded them all up? The Sheepeaters were always too smart for us.

Unhandy terrain for chasing Indians.

Photo by Ernest E. Day
Courtesy Idaho Historical Society

Chapter 22

THE McBETH SISTERS AND "THE MEASURING WOMAN"

O NE OF THE fascinating things about history is the unexpected people you run into in the most unlikely places. Years before Idaho became a State, several intellectual spinsters from the East, showed up in the activities of North Idaho.

After the country simmered down from the Civil War, and we had succeeded in penning up all the Indians on reservations, our Government began to suffer pangs of conscience over the way we had treated the original inhabitants of America. The way we were still treating them, for that matter, because many Indian Agents in charge of reservations, were pulling some pretty slick tricks to line their own pockets at the expense of the Indians they were supposed to protect.

The churches had been crying out for years about our un-Christian treatment of our brothers. Finally, President Grant divided the seventy reservations among the various churches, to see what they could do in the way of education. The Presbyterian Mission Board was made responsible for the Nez Perce, because it had established the original mission at Lapwai, under the Reverend Henry Spalding.

In 1873, the Board sent out Miss Sue McBeth, to teach with Reverend Spalding, who had returned to the mission in his old age.

Miss McBeth was a very unusual woman. She had been born by the River Doon in Scotland. She had taught among the Choctaw Indians in Oklahoma Territory until the Civil War, and then she had tended the sick and dying soldiers. After the war she became a city missionary in St. Louis, which was a very tough city. Then she returned to teaching in a college in Fairfield, Iowa. Now for twenty years she would live under primitive conditions in Kamiah and Mount Idaho, dedicating the rest of her life to educating Indians to live in a white man's world.

This was no easy task. The chiefs, particularly the popular Chief Joseph, were her bitter enemies. She believed the Indians must learn to think of themselves as individuals, instead of just part of a band; and to accomplish this, she believed the power of the chiefs over their people must be destroyed.

Miss Sue McBeth.
Courtesy Idaho Historical Society

Miss Kate McBeth.
Courtesy Idaho Historical Society

The Indian Agent at Lapwai also made her work difficult. He didn't approve of women missionaries and their ideas.

About a month before the Nez Perce War broke out, General Howard, stationed at Fort Lapwai, paid Miss McBeth a visit at her home in Mount Idaho. He was greatly impressed by this frail woman with the fine mind and the indomitable spirit. Her health had been damaged by the conditions under which she had nursed in the Civil War, and she had some crippling kind of paralysis that made her partially an invalid, but she paid very little attention to pain and discomfort. "Her home is very simple," General Howard wrote. "She has a lounge and a chair, and in another room there is a cabinet organ and a few benches. Miss McBeth gathers her students about her, a few at a time, and instructs them to become teachers."

Six years after Sue arrived in Idaho, she was joined by her younger sister, Kate.

Sue worked with the young Indian men, preparing them for teaching and the ministry, while Kate worked with the women. For twenty-seven years she taught them, a little writing, spelling, arithmetic, geography, singing, and much Bible reading. She taught them practical skills, such as making soap from grease and lye, baking, and knitting.

Indian women had no more standing than a slave, but the desire of some of them for accomplishment was very great. The organization of a missionary society, Kate regarded as a great triumph. The women yearned to try it, but they knew the men would make fun of them—"women bosses" trying to be officers of an organization! They went ahead after awhile, and we can imagine how much courage it must have taken, in the face of their husbands' jeers. They became devoted to their missionary society, and wouldn't think of missing a meeting, no matter what the weather or the difficulty. They sewed warm under-garments for the old women. They made beadwork to be sold by missionery groups in the East, and with the proceeds they bought seats and a bell for their church, and presented them with great pride.

A many-years project of Miss Sue McBeth was the making of a Nez Perce dictionary and grammar, which is now in the Smithsonian Institution. This manuscript had a strange adventure on its journey to the Smithsonian, after Miss McBeth's death. Kate took it to Lewiston to ship by the Union Pacific. It would go the first part of its journey down the Snake River by boat.

This was the trip on which the boat, "Annie Faxon," blew up, killing or injuring everyone on board, and scattering its cargo over the river. A young farmer living beside the Snake River some miles

Miss Alice Fletcher, "The Measuring Woman."

Courtesy Idaho Historical Society

below the explosion, saw a red box floating past his farm. He rode horseback as far out into the river as he could, and lassoed the box just as it was going over some rapids. When he opened it, he recognized the Nez Perce script on the soaked pages.

He had once lived at Lapwai and was acquainted with the McBeth sisters. He and his wife, with great care, separated the pages and laid them to dry. A Union Pacific express agent, tracing the shipment, arrived to take charge of the damaged manuscript, and get it delivered to the Smithsonian.

The sisters are buried in the cemetery behind the old Nez Perce church at Kamiah they loved so well. The church's notice slate still announces the hours of its Sunday services. The graves are easy to find, for around them is built one of those old-fashioned iron picket fences. Also in the enclosure is the grave of the Reverend Robert Williams, their first ordained Nez Perce pastor and a loyal friend and helper of the McBeth sisters. I must admit that it set me back a little, to find that the grave of his wife, although parallel and in line with her husband's grave, is outside that picket fence of distinction! Today we would complain of discrimination.

The old Nez Perce Presbyterian Church and graveyard at Kamiah.

Courtesy Idaho Dept. Tourism and Industrial Development

The next thing the Government set about, to ease its conscience and convert Indians from tribes to individuals, was to allot individual acreages out of the reservation lands. This undertaking was also entrusted to the sponsorship of the church mission boards.

In 1889, two New England women arrived at Kamiah to headquarter in the uncomfortable old mission house while they worked at allotting land to the Nez Perce Indians. Miss Alice Fletcher, fifty years old, had been appointed by President Harrison as Allotment Agent for the Nez Perce. She was completely dedicated to the welfare of the Indians. Miss Jane Gay, sixty years old, was completely dedicated to the welfare of her friend Alice, and also served as photographer for the undertaking. For four hot, dusty summers, accompanied by a surveyor and any number of Indians, they jolted and jounced over the rough trails in a wagon driven by a young Nez Perce.

At the first rumor that the U.S. Government had thought up something new to benefit them, the Indians got their backs up. They stared at Miss Fletcher with cold suspicion. They had had a good deal of experience with Government benefits.

But Miss Alice Fletcher was an unusual woman. She was kindly, she was patient, there was no limit to the trouble she would go to, to secure for an Indian the piece of land he wanted, with good soil and a spring of good water. In the end, the honesty of her good will endeared her to them. Even Chief Joseph, who bitterly resented the McBeth sisters for downgrading the authority of the chiefs, rode horseback 150 miles from the Colville Agency in Washington to visit with Miss Fletcher after hearing the favorable reports of his friends. She tried to persuade him to take an allotment to which he was entitled, in Idaho. But he was an old man, past the energy to start over. The Colville reservation included some pleasant country. He finished out his life where he was.

When the allotment work was finished and Miss Fletcher returned to Washington, D. C., three commissioners instantly appeared in North Idaho to buy the surplus, unallotted land. Each Indian was paid a proportionate share for the surplus land, but many would have preferred that the tribe keep it for horse and cattle pasture, or for future generations.

A small number of gamblers and drinkers among the Nez Perce went through their money in a hurry, but most made good use of it. They paid off debts, built houses and barns, and bought tools and sewing machines.

The Nez Perce demonstrated their confidence in their "Measuring Woman" for years afterward. If any trouble should arise about a cornerstone or a line fence, they would say, "Is Miss Fletcher still in Washington? Tell her this and that, and ask her to go to the Office about it," and Miss Fletcher would proceed to take care of it.

Chapter 23

A MERRY HEART FROM CHINA

IDAHO HISTORY IS long on men, short on women. It isn't that the women weren't here, but they were so busy building homes, raising families, bringing civilization to the raw frontier, they didn't have time left over to impress themselves on history.

I want to tell you about one Idaho woman who became famous in a small way, not because she did anything historical, but because she brought warmth and humanness to a time and place that was often bleak and brutal.

Her name was Lalu Nathoy. She was born in 1853, in the north of China near the Mongolian border, where brigands for centuries had been sweeping down to raid the countryside. Lalu's family was very poor, farming a small plot of ground, and when they weren't suffering from the plundering of brigands, their crop was burning up with drought. There came a year of great famine, when there was not only drought, but the outlaws galloped out of the north and stripped the farmers of what little grain there was, leaving them destitute.

To keep the rest of the family from starving, Lalu's father traded her to the brigands in exchange for enough seed to plant another crop. She was sold to an outfit that shipped women slaves to the New World. Lalu was 18 when she arrived on the West Coast.

All Chinese in this country were controlled by an organization of wealthy San Francisco Chinese called the "Six Companies." They sold Lalu, she claimed, for $2,500 to "an old Chinee-man," Hong King, who took her and two other Chinese girls with his pack train to Warren, Idaho, where he owned a saloon and dancehall. The other girls were soon moved to another mining camp, but Lalu remained in Warren to work as a dancehall hostess. She lived in Warren for the next 23 years.

Everybody liked her. She was a lively, cheerful young girl. When people had trouble with her Chinese name, they christened her Polly; a name that was lively and cheerful like herself. Polly she was for the rest of her long life.

Polly was never idle for an hour. She did a lot of the work in the saloon, and when there was sickness in camp, she was called out

Polly Bemis.

for nursing. She was small and quick. Later, when she lived in the country, people said she ran up and down and whisked around the hills like a squirrel in a pine tree.

She liked to crochet and whenever she had a free moment, her crochet hook was flying. Somewhere she picked up the craft of gold-smithing, and when she could beg a gold nugget, she would hammer it into miniature gold-pans, picks, or hammers, to sell for jewelry. She never learned to read or write, but she was bright as a dollar, and had a remarkable memory. She could tell you the name and birth date of every child born in Warren, and the date of every death.

Next door to Hong King's saloon was another saloon, owned by Charlie Bemis. Charlie had come west from Connecticut with his father to work a claim, but he was inclined to be lazy, and soon found he would rather run a saloon and gambling hall than dig for gold. On his violin he played old tunes he carried in his head. A man named Peter Bemer, who must have had considerable knowledge of music, took down the notes most skillfully, making a book of the tunes to be played for dances. A reproduction of this book is in the Idaho Historical Museum.

Charlie and Polly Bemis at "The Polly Place."
Courtesy Idaho Historical Society

Charlie Bemis was a kindly man and he became a friend to Polly. She needed a friend. Mining camps were wild and rough, especially the saloons. Whenever Hong King's saloon got too rough for her, Polly would dash out the back door and, in her guttural Chinese voice, holler for Bemis. He always came to her rescue. He was young himself, only a few years older than Polly, but he was a quiet, stern man, with a reputation with a six-shooter that cooled down the rowdies.

Bemis was liked and trusted in the town. Miners starting on a drinking binge often brought him their hoards of gold dust for safekeeping until they would be sober again. One night, when Polly had been in Warren almost twenty years, a man named Johnny Cox handed Bemis $150 in gold dust to keep for him, telling him to be sure not to return it until he was stone sober, even if he begged for it. Later, rolling drunk, Johnny returned and demanded the gold. Bemis tried to put him off. Angered, Johnny said he would give him time to roll a cigarette, then if he didn't hand it over, he would shoot out his eye. As Bemis still tried to stall, Johnny suddenly raised his revolver and fired. His aim was not steady and the bullet missed the eye, instead entering Bemis' cheek and traveling downward to lodge in his neck.

They sent for a doctor at Grangeville. It was a long, hard ride to Warren, more than a hundred miles through the mountains, and the doctor was good and tired when he arrived. He was also good and tired of the careless ways of miners with guns. He examined the ugly wound, said grumpily it was sure to prove fatal and there wasn't much he could do about it, collected $500 and headed back for Grangeville.

Polly was indignant for her friend and she took over the case. She removed the bullet from his neck with the help of a razor, cleaned out the festered wound with her crochet hook (sterilized, no doubt, with whisky), and nursed him back to health.

Charlie Bemis was an incurable gambler. He couldn't stop playing as long as he had one thing left to bet. In a poker game with Hong King he lost all his money, and finally bet his saloon against a little gold, and Hong King's slave girl. Charlie won.

After that, Polly ran a boarding-house at Charlie's place. She was an excellent cook. She was the kind of woman who soon becomes indispensable, especially to a lazy man with a business. There was also some danger of her being deported to China, since she had no papers. Four years after he won her at poker, Charlie decided to marry her.

They were married in 1894, when Polly was 41 and Charlie was 46. Two years later, Polly was issued her "Certificate of Residence for Chinese Laborer" by the U.S. Government. This and her marriage certificate were her proudest possessions. You can see them today at the museum at St. Gertrude's Convent.

Take a few hours sometime and drive to the convent, in the lovely countryside, a few miles from Cottonwood. Find Sister Alfreda Elsensohn, if you can to escort you through the museum. Sister Alfreda, a native of Grangeville, is a Benedictine nun and teacher, and is also an Idaho historian and the author of several books. It was she who started and has developed St. Gertrude's Museum, and she is its loving curator.

She will show you a cupboardful of Polly's things. Besides the two proud certificates, there is a very pretty photo of her at the time of her marriage, and there are several kodak snapshots. Some handsome wedding silverware that speaks of the regard of friends, some jewelry, three dresses and a sunbonnet, a shawl, some of her crochet work and pieces of her goldsmithing. Sister Alfreda is grieved that she once left the cupboard unlocked when some young boys were in the museum unattended, and gold coin buttons made by Polly, disappeared.

Charlie Bemis' health was not good and he decided to try a more peaceful way of life. He bought some land at the edge of the Salmon River, forty miles upriver from Riggins, reached only by boat. At first people called it the "Bemis place," but before long it became the "Polly place."

And there was no doubt who was boss. Finding Charlie playing cribbage with neighbors, Polly would count up to fifteen, then issue her ultimatum: "You go home, put wood in woodbox." And Charlie would go. Finding him leisurely studying a nest of ants, she pointed out, "Bemis, if you work um like these ants, we wouldn't be poor folks." She always spoke in the pidgin English she learned when she first came to America.

Polly loved their ranch on the river. She hiked around with Charlie on his hunting trips because her eyes were sharper than his. She became an expert fisherwoman. The canyon was thousands of feet deep, mostly too steep for farming. But on fifteen acres at the base of the canyon Polly raised cherries, pears, plums, grapes, blackberries, strawberries, watermelons, vegetables, and clover. Her farm childhood stayed with her; she had the true green thumb.

Charlie's health kept worsening and by 1919, he was an invalid. Across the river was the ranch of Charles Shepp and Peter Klinkhammer, who became the most loyal friends the Bemis couple had, watching over them for the rest of their lives. They strung a telephone line the half-mile from their ranch across the river to the "Polly place," and checked on them regularly. Polly dearly loved the telephone. If her neighbors failed to call her, she would call them. "How many eggs you get today? Six? I get 10!" and she would go off into gales of giggles. "How many fish you catch? None? You no good.

You fella come over Sunday, I cook great big fish I catch today."

Cissie Patterson, a newspaper woman from a famous newspaper family, and herself to become owner of the Washington Times Herald, came west and took a boat trip down the Salmon, "River of No Return," and met Polly at her home. It speaks for Polly's quality that this sophisticated and fashionable woman was enchanted with her. "Five feet tall, she is brown and wrinkled as a nut," she wrote, "and at 69, is full of dash and charm."

In 1922, the Bemis house caught fire and burned to the ground. Polly and the neighbors from across the river got Charlie safely out, but they saved very little else. Two months later, Charlie died. Polly moved back to Warren for the winter.

In the spring her good neighbors built a new log house on her ranch, and bed, chairs, and table. She was now nearly seventy years old, and she made an agreement with them that if they would watch out for her, she would deed her property to them. They took care of her heavy gardening, and provided her with wood and game. And since she couldn't read or write, Shepp's diary constantly noted, "Ordered garden seeds for Polly," and "Measured Polly for dress and ordered from Montgomery-Ward."

In 1923, friends took Polly on a trip to Grangeville. She had her first ride in an automobile, she saw a train and her first movie, and she came home with a new dress, hat and white shoes. The next year they took her to Boise, a "big city." Polly stayed at the Idanha Hotel, rode in an elevator, and saw the sights. "Yes, I like it," she said, "but it makes me tired to look so much."

Polly Bemis lived out her four score years and was buried in a Grangeville plot, so many thousand miles across an ocean from the plot where she was born.

If you should sometime come across that grave, will you stop and give a moment's thought to the peasant girl who accepted whatever life dealt her and went ahead to build happiness on it. She is something to think about.

Chapter 24

IDAHO EUZKALDUNAK

FEW AMERICANS had heard of the Basque people before the California gold rush. Even today they are one of the mysteries of history. Their homeland is in seven provinces in the Pyrenees Mountains, on both sides of the boundary between Spain and France, and they have lived right there for thousands of years. Nobody knows where they came from. Their language does not resemble any other language we know.

The Atlantic Ocean touches their homeland, and they have always been great seafarers and fishermen. A shipload of Basques actually beat Columbus to America, hunting codfish around Newfoundland. Columbus's navigator, Lakotza, was a Basque. Another Basque, Elkano, took command of the ship when Magellan was murdered by Filipinos, and he completed that first circumnavigation of the world.

When gold was discovered in California, and silver in Nevada, the Basques began to arrive. They didn't have a lot of luck with gold, so they had to hunt around the West for jobs to keep from starving. The biggest problem was not being able to talk to people who weren't Basque. English was so different from their own language, it was very difficult for them to learn. (Do you know the story about the young Basque, just arrived in Mountain Home, who ate every day in the same restaurant so he could pick up some English words from the friendly owners? After two weeks he hadn't learned a single word. Then a friend informed him that it was a Chinese restaurant, and the owners couldn't speak English either!)

The sheep industry was growing into a big business in the West just then, and the ranchers were desperate for good herders. The sociable Americans couldn't stand the lonely work, and Indians and Mexicans hadn't proved very conscientious about taking care of sheep. The ranchers tried out a few of these Basque strangers who couldn't speak English. As it happened, some of these young Basques had never seen a sheep before. At home in their provinces in Spain and France they worked as fishermen, or in shipyards, or iron mines, or rope factories. To everybody's surprise, they turned out to be among the world's best herders. They had been raised with a strong sense of duty. They would stay with a flock through a blizzard, rather than abandon it to save their own lives. Sheep, with a Basque herder, came through a season fatter, stronger, produced better lambs, and gave richer milk. A Basque was clever about getting the very best use out of range land—even, sometimes, a bit illegally. There was once a Basque herder who took the bells off his sheep at night, and turned them into the wonderful grass that grew at the Idaho State Penitentiary!

Basque sheepherder

Courtesy Idaho Dept. of Tourism and Industrial Development

In the 1890s, Boise really began to grow, as a center for stock ranches. Word went back to the Basque homeland that there was plenty of work in Idaho. Times were hard in the provinces, and the young men began to leave by the hundreds, heading for Idaho and

Nevada. Can you imagine them, boys who had never traveled fifty miles from home, getting on a ship to cross the Atlantic Ocean, and then taking their first train ride 3,000 miles from New York to Boise? They carried all their belongings on their back, or in a battered family suitcase tied with a rope, and their mothers had packed a parcel of bread and strong-smelling chorizo sausages for them to eat on the way. Long after he arrived here, one young fellow told a story on himself that you can believe or not, but it makes a good story: His mother had warned him to guard his religious faith because "America was a heathen kind of country." He wrote her that she needn't worry, many people on the train had prayed all day; he could see their lips moving. It was only later he found they were chewing gum, a new thing in his experience! Basques have a great sense of humor, and can nearly always laugh at themselves.

The first years here must have been terrible for those young boys. They usually arrived from Spain to go to work in lambing time, and when lambing was over, they were given a dog and a band of sheep, and headed for the hills to spend the next six or eight months. They were used to hard work, but not to working alone. They had grown up amidst a lively neighborhood life—many feast days, dancing, games and good wine. Now their only companionship was the stars, a dog, and 2,500 sheep! You have heard the saying, "Crazy as a sheepherder," and you can well imagine that many of them would truly become peculiar from desperate loneliness.

Sheep owners did not encourage their herders to learn English, because then they could go into other kinds of work, and they didn't want to lose their valuable hands. In 1911, a Basque priest, the Reverend Bernardo Arregui, came from Spain to live in Idaho and take care of the religious needs of his people. He rode horseback great distances through the hills, visiting the herders; and that made their lives a little more endurable.

The earliest Basques in Idaho were all men. They didn't intend to stay; they would earn some money and take it home. But there wasn't much future for them at home, and some of them could see the possibilities in this new, young country. The more enterprising among them began to acquire a few sheep of their own, and before many years, Idaho had developed a number of "sheep kings" who were Basque—John Archabal, Antone Uranga, Miguel Gabica, Jose Bengoechia, Joe Uberuaga, Antonio Azcuenaga, Jose Navarro. (It is interesting that the tongue-twisting Basque names all have a meaning. "Echevarria," which is as common among Basques as "Smith" is among us, means "new house." "Mendiola" means "wood from the mountain." "Bideganeta" means "top of the road."

When those early herders came to town, they kept to their own people, with whom they could talk. Several Basque boardinghouses, with their need for cooks and housekeepers, brought Basque women from their homeland to Idaho. Men began to send back home for wives and sweethearts, and families started settling down in Idaho towns. Basques were well-supplied with brothers and sisters, and uncles and aunts and cousins, and gradually a lot of them followed the first emigrants to this land. Hundreds came between 1900 and 1920. Then Congress restricted the number of people who could come each year from the countries of southern Europe. All Spain has a quota of only 250 people a year. But the sheep ranchers complained loudly of their need for Basque herders, until Congress passed special laws to permit a certain number of Basques to come into the United States for a three-year stay, provided they herded sheep. However, hundreds of other young Basques signed on as ships' crews, and jumped ships in American ports.

Now there are between 6,000 and 7,000 Basque descendants living in the Boise Valley. Hardly any of them are sheepherders any more. They have gone into every occupation.

A few years ago, the Ambassador from Spain (who, since World War II, has always been Basque) stated with pride that there was not a single case of a Basque in this country with a criminal record. However, in the last few years, I have noticed in the newspapers a few Basque names in brushes with the law, so I assume that our Basques have now become totally Americanized.

They are proud of their Basque heritage. Especially since the Civil War in Spain in 1939 crushed the Basque provinces and stamped out their ancient liberties, our Basques in the United States have redoubled their efforts to keep their traditions alive. Boise State University has lately added a course in the Basque language, so that younger generations will not lose it completely. Nearly all Idahoans, whether Euzkaldunak or other nationality, by now must have enjoyed the swift and strenuous dance group known as the "Oinkari," which means "fast feet." They performed at World Fairs in both New York and Seattle, and take part in folk dance festivals all over the country. Their music is played on a drum, an accordion, a tambourine, and a kind of flute-fife, the "txistu."

All Basque recreations are strenuous. Every year they hold game competitions in weight-lifting, weight-pulling, and woodchopping. There used to be courts here for the madly violent kind of basket handball called pelota, or jai alai (pronounced "hi-a-li") but that seems to be a thing of the past. Younger generations have switched to American football and baseball.

Have you ever heard the Basque "War Cry?" Sometimes, one of the dancers, in the speed and excitement of a dance, gets carried

Oinkari dancers ready for the hoop dance.

Courtesy Idaho Dept. of Tourism and Industrial Development

away and turns loose with it. It was developed in the homeland to carry from one Pyrenees peak to another, and you can well imagine it would. It has been described as combining a horse's neigh, a wolf's howl, and a jackass's bray, and it ends in a truly blood-chilling screech. It is said it struck terror to the hearts of Napoleon's tough soldiers in the dark of the night, when they were invading Spain— and I can well believe it did.

Governor Frank Steunenberg statue which faces Idaho Capitol Building.

Photo by Duane Garrett

Chapter 25

IDAHO'S FAMOUS TRIAL

WE DON'T THINK of Idaho as being much of a Labor state. Our main activities are farming and stock ranching. But at the turn of the century there was a bitter war between miners and mine owners in North Idaho that ended in an assassination and a trial that stirred up violent feeling all over the United States and Europe. The symbol that reminds us of that violent time is the statue of Frank Steunenberg, which stands facing our capitol building. (You may have noticed that the statue is tie-less. It is said that the Governor never in his life wore a necktie.)

The Coeur d'Alene mines had hardly gotten into big production before the country was hit by the great depression of the 1890s. Banks closed all over the country and businesses failed. At the mines the price for lead and silver dropped, but freight rates did not. Some of the mines closed down. The mine operators cut wages.

In those days workers had no rights. Rights were all on the side of employers. A worker took what he was given and smothered his complaints. With this one-sided power, and anger bottled up in thousands of workers, it was only a question of time till something exploded.

Samuel Gompers, a dynamic little Jewish immigrant, tried to do something about such injustice. If the workers could join together, the strength of numbers would be on their side. In 1886, he organized skilled workers into craft unions under the American Federation of Labor, to work for better pay, better hours, and better working conditions. He would have nothing to do with radical ideas or politics or violent action. In what was a liberal field of activity, he was a conservative. It was certain that not all workers were going to be satisfied with such mild improvements in the American work situation. Some of the more aggressive members of a local miners' union in the Coeur d'Alene area began to develop a more belligerent organization, calling it the Western Federation of Miners. When they started signing up members, the alarmed mine operators began to fight them. The miners went out on strike. The mine operators brought in strikebreakers, Pinkerton detectives and private armies. The miners set up picket lines and there were broken heads. The battle went on for years.

The climax came on April 29, 1899. In an action as carefully planned as a military operation, the union men ran the strike-breakers out of Bunker Hill and Sullivan's concentrator mill at Wardner and blew the mill to kindling.

The plan went off like clockwork. An armed guard of union men commandeered a Northern Pacific train at Burke and ran it the twenty miles to Wardner, loaded with 4,500 pounds of dynamite. More than a thousand union men, most wearing masks so they couldn't be identified, and some armed with rifles, marched double-file up the canyon. They drove out the strikebreakers, set three charges of powder, blew up the mill, took the train back to Burke, and went home to supper. One strikebreaker had been killed.

Strikers cut the telegraph lines, but word got through somehow to Governor Steunenberg in Boise. The Governor did not hesitate. Frank Steunenberg was a quiet, friendly, unassuming man, but a man of very strong character, with a stern sense of duty.

He was a union man himself, having belonged since a young man, to a printers' craft union and his newspaper (The Caldwell Tribune) was pro-Labor. But as Governor he would not permit a union's name to shield lawlessness. His first loyalty was to the law and the State of Idaho.

He would normally have sent the Idaho National Guard to restore order, but our Guard was then in the Philippines fighting in the Spanish-American War, so the Governor called on President McKinley to send in Federal troops. They were sent over from the military fort at Spokane, and they did restore order, but they were of course very unpopular. They rounded up several hundred miners and kept them under guard in a stockade people called the "bullpen," until they would sign a statement giving up membership in the union.

Martial law always leaves a bad taste, and those responsible are hated. At the end of Governor Steunenberg's term, his political life was over. He didn't mind. He was content to return to private business in Caldwell.

At the turn of the century there was developing in our nation a new conscience about the underdog. People were beginning to de-mand that something be done for our poverty-stricken workers, the unskilled laborers in mills, mines, railroads. They were usually immigrants and often could not even speak English. They were not eligible to join craft unions, and there was nothing to protect them from employers who might work them ten-, twelve-, and fourteen-hour days, and pay them barely enough to keep their families alive.

In 1905, divergent groups came together in a meeting in Chicago to try to figure out some way to help them. Many of the groups might not have much else in common, and even objected to each other, but they all did hate the unjust system under which workers made a poor living.

There was the newly organized Socialist political party, led by the gentle, idealistic Eugene Debs. There was the Western Federation of Miners, led by tough Big Bill Haywood. There was only one woman, 75-year-old Mother Mary Jones, who had lost her husband and four children in a cholera epidemic, and would spend the rest of her hundred years picketing and agitating for coal miners and mill workers, and fighting against child labor.

Big Bill Haywood, a Western Federation power from Silver City mines, had been one of the moving spirits in setting up the meeting, and he was elected chairman. He was an effective speaker and could make men follow him, and what he preached was the necessity of using any weapon to reach their goals—strikes, violence, terrorism, politics.

So the Industrial Workers of the World was born—an organization, not of crafts, but of whole industries—mines, railroads, textile mills—taking in all workers, skilled and unskilled. Its constitution declared against any peace between workers and employers. Total war to attain better conditions for workers.

The I.W.W.s (nicknamed the "Wobblies") inspired terrific enthusiasm among unskilled workers who had never had anybody to take their part. They brought out a lot of lively, stirring songs that became popular all over the country. When I was in high school, one of our favorite tunes was "Hallelujah! I'm a Bum!" and I doubt if, at that time, I had heard of the I.W.W.s.

The I.W.W. declared any weapons were justified to attain their ends, and any weapons were pretty much what they used. Strikes, riots, and a certain amount of more violent activities against management and strike breakers. And in a few instances, they got even with somebody for past actions to which they objected.

It was on December 30, 1905, six years after the dynamiting of the Wardner mill that the union got even with ex-Governor Frank Steunenberg.

It was Saturday night. A life insurance agent had telephoned Mr. Steunenberg that morning to tell him that his life insurance policy would expire that day. He would be at the Saratoga Hotel all day, he said, if Mr. Steunenberg would like to drop by and renew it. It happened that Mrs. Steunenberg had recently joined the Seventh Day Adventist Church and the family observed Saturday as their Sabbath, until after sundown. Mr. Steunenberg explained this to the agent, and said he would come to the hotel in the evening.

He did so, paid the renewal on his policy, visited a bit with acquaintances in the lobby, and walked back home. On the way he passed a man hurrying in the opposite direction, but the man was a stranger and he paid no attention to him. He opened the gate in the picket fence around his yard and was blown to pieces by a bomb wired to it.

Within 48 hours the murder was traced to a stranger called Tom Hogan who had been staying at the hotel for the last two months, claiming to be a sheep-buyer although he never bought any sheep. He was a friendly, pleasant man, easy to get acquainted with, and at first the police simply couldn't believe he could be the murderer.

However, Sheriff Harvey Brown of Baker, Oregon, a former miner, happened to be in Caldwell on business, and he recognized Harry Orchard from Coeur d'Alene days. (And thereby signed his own death sentence: nearly two years later, when he was scheduled to appear as witness in the trial of another I.W.W. hatchet-man, Sheriff Brown opened the gate of his home in Baker and was blown to bits by the explosion of a bomb. The I.W.W. had a long memory.)

For some reason, Orchard did not leave town immediately after Steunenberg's murder. While he was wandering the Caldwell streets, the police searched his hotel room and found all kinds of evidence. There was a satchel containing fuse, caps, sugar, chloride of potash, plaster of Paris, wire, screw eyes, flashlight and a gun. In a trunk checked at the depot they found sticks of dynamite, a sawed-off shotgun, several disguises, and a collection of burglar tools. (All of these items, used as evidence in Orchard's trial, are in the possession of the Idaho Historical Society.)

The police of a small country town like Caldwell, confronted with a political assassination, didn't know how to proceeed. They kept Orchard in their jail for eighteen days and then by arrangement with the State of Idaho, moved him to the penitentiary where he was put in solitary confinement until they could make up their minds what to do.

Orchard maintained his innocence, and in all his career of previous crimes he had never been arrested and had no police record. It was the general opinion, locally, that he was only the tool of higher-ups, but it would be a very difficult thing to prove.

James McParland, western manager of the Pinkerton Detective Agency, was brought to Boise from Denver, and set himself to win a confession from the prisoner. He had done a lot of work for mine operators in ferreting out union agitators and hatchet-men, and had been successful thirty years before in getting confessions out of members of the secret "Molly McGuire" organization at the time of the Pennsylvania coal mine violence.

McParland was a persuasive man, a charming, musical-voiced Irishman of almost no education, but high intelligence.

McParland visited Orchard a few times in his solitary cell, talking sympathetically, pointing out how unjust it would be for Orchard to be convicted of the crime while his employers went free.

These talks had an effect on Orchard. He enjoyed company and the solitary confinement wore him down. McParland learned that as a boy, Orchard had been required to attend Sunday School by his religious mother. On one of his visits he handed Orchard a religious tract, saying, "It was left here for you by the widow of the man you murdered." He also set up a phonograph within hearing of Orchard's cell, and played records of hymns.

In the end he won him over. Orchard told him the story of his entire life, as ugly a story as you could hear.

He was born Albert Horsley on a poor, small farm in Ontario, Canada. He went to a country school through third grade, and then went to work on neighboring farms, and later in logging camps.

Albert made friends easily, and he had a natural talent for business. He might easily have lived a successful, respectable life. But there was a kink in his character that made him prefer easy money, however he could get it. He would go along as a good citizen for quite a while, and then he would pull something crooked and get into trouble. Finally he abandoned his wife and child, threw up his business, and went out West, ending up at the Coeur d'Alene mines in Idaho.

He didn't care much for hard work, and for awhile he took odd jobs like delivering milk and hauling wood. For $500 he bought a one-sixteenth share in a mining prospect in Burke Canyon. He didn't want to do any digging, of course, and in a short time he sold his interest for a small profit. If he had held onto it, in 1901 he would have found himself one-sixteenth owner of the fabulous Hercules silver and lead mine, which produced $100,000,000!

The officers of the Western Federation of Miners must have recognized the kink in his character, for presently they approached him with a proposition to work for them, and sent him off to be trained in the use of dynamite.

He became a hatchet-man for the union, and was very successful on several jobs in the Coeur d'Alene area. In the Cripple Creek mining district of Colorado, he dynamited a train station platform when it was crowded with non-union men, killing 65 and maiming more than 100.

Orchard admitted to McParland that he had murdered Steunen-

Harry Orchard at time of trial, 1907.

Courtesy Idaho Historical Society

berg. He had done it, he said, under the orders of the executive board of the Western Federation of Miners, who were also officers of the I.W.W.—Charles Moyer, William Haywood, and George Pettibone.

The headquarters of these men was Denver. They would not, of course, have been in Idaho at the time of the bombing. Extradition from Colorado to stand trial in Idaho was going to be very ticklish. Let word get out, and the leaders could simply fade into hiding. With all the miners in Colorado to protect them, they would be impossible to find.

The authorities in Idaho and Colorado went quietly, cautiously to work. Some of the most murderous activities of the union had taken place in Colorado, and feeling against the leaders ran high in government circles there. Acting on the shaky legal premise that all conspirators to a crime can be considered present at the scene of the crime, the governor of Colorado signed papers for the arrest of the three union officers.

The arresting officers held the papers until Saturday night when the courts were closed for the weekend and habeas corpus action would not be obtainable. The men were awakened in the night and served with the warrants. They were taken one by one before dawn Sunday to the Denver depot. A special train was waiting, steam up and curtains drawn, under an armed guard headed by Deputy Warden J. C. Mills of the Idaho State Penitentiary. The train took off for Idaho, with only brief, prearranged halts to take on water, and early Monday morning it pulled into Boise, where the prisoners were whisked off to the penitentiary.

Instantly a howl went up all over the country over the "kidnapping." The unions demanded the immediate release of their leaders. They filed the case with the courts, and it went all the way to the Supreme Court, delaying the trials for over a year. The Supreme Court finally ruled that although the arrests might not have been strictly legal, once in Idaho the men could be tried for Steuncnberg's murder.

William Haywood would be the first man tried because there was the most evidence against him. The unions hired Clarence Darrow, who had long been associated with labor and civil liberties cases, to defend him. Darrow was a brilliant trial lawyer from Chicago, on his way up. He had a great sense of the dramatic.

Under old-hand, James Hawley, for the prosecution, was a rising young lawyer with some of the same dramatic qualities as Darrow. William E. Borah had just been elected to the U.S. Senate, but he would not begin serving there until this trial was over.

Borah had recently achieved local fame in the trial against Paul Corcoran for the shooting of the strikebreaker at the time of the Wardner mill dynamiting. Corcoran's alibi had been that he was miles away at the time the man was shot. Witnesses, however, swore they saw him riding on top of the commandeered train, carrying a rifle, and that he had jumped off the train as it went through Burke.

The conductor and the brakeman testified this would have been impossible; with the speed of the train, and the rough and crooked roadbed, a man standing on the train would have been thrown off and killed. Thereupon, young Borah, duplicating the original conditions and carrying a rifle, rode the same route on top of a car, and jumped off at Burke, landing on his feet!

With two such men as Darrow and Borah on opposing sides of the trial, there would be plenty of excitement.

And seldom have Americans been so aroused over a civil liberties' case. The extradition proceedings, no doubt about it, looked suspiciously like a frame-up. Even the gentle Eugene Debs, who had vowed that Socialism must be a peaceful movement within the nation's legal framework, and who hated the violence of the I.W.W.s, nevertheless now wrote in a passionate fury against the kidnapping. If the courts sentenced Moyer, Haywood and Pettibone to die, Debs declared that a million revolutionists would march with guns. This brought down denunciations on his head from every conservative newspaper in the country.

There was an amusing sequel later, when Debs toured the Northwest to raise money for the defense. He planned to go to Boise after a rally in Pocatello, but a telegram came from his old friend, Clarence Darrow. It read, "For the sake of Moyer, Pettibone and Haywood, please stay away from Boise. I will have enough trouble acquitting them of murder without having the added burden of acquitting them of Socialism." Deeply wounded, Debs boarded a train for home.

Samuel Gompers, no friend of Haywood, nevertheless, rose at the 1906 convention of the A. F. of L. to denounce the Colorado and Idaho authorities for the kidnapping.

Twenty thousand New Yorkers showed up at Grand Central Station to listen to a speech on injustice by a Socialist leader. The newspaper "Appeal to Reason" published a special edition of a million copies. In Boston, 50,000 workers and their families, marched through the streets collecting money for the defense, while bands played the Marseillaise. That stirring song of the bloody French Revolution became, overnight, the song of the angry workers, and marching men chanted, "If Moyer and Haywood die, If Moyer and Haywood die, Twenty million workers will know the reason why." Contributions from 25 cents to $1,000 came from workers everywhere for the defense.

President Theodore Roosevelt added to the general hurrah by announcing flatly that Eugene Debs, Moyer and Haywood were "undesirable citizens." This was naturally taken up with high spirits by thousands of college students, who began wearing buttons on their lapels proclaiming, "I am an Undesirable Citizen."

The first task Darrow set himself was to weaken the effect of Orchard's confession. To have standing in court, it must be backed by other evidence. A second confession, won by Detective McParland from Steve Adams, another union hatchet-man, had corroborated a good deal of Orchard's testimony, and the prosecution counted heavily on it. But now Darrow, working as skillfully as McParland had done, succeeded in getting Adams to say he had lied about the whole thing to save his own skin. This was a great blow to the prosecution.

Eighteen months after the murder, the trial of Haywood began. The quiet streets of Boise were alive with strangers. Reporters from every large city in the United States, journalists from England and Russia, Socialists, reformers, lawyers, magazine writers, filled every hotel and boardinghouse.

On the morning of May 9, 1907, in court behind Haywood sat his mother, his invalid wife, and his two little girls. The stage was set. The trial got under way.

Despite the loss of Steve Adams' testimony, Orchard's story was very damaging to the defendants. He never changed his story, he told it in a most convincing manner, and he never tried to excuse himself. People could abhor the kind of man he was, but they believed his story.

The trial lasted nearly three months. Newspapers everywhere kept it boiling. The Socialist Party, the unions and the workers took it as a foregone conclusion that the men would be convicted. Radical newspapers insisted that the trial was "fixed" beforehand. They said the judge was an arch-conservative whose mind was already made up, that the jury was composed of farmers and small ranchers, some of them friends of Steunenberg (which was true), and they would not judge the case with open minds. The system was against them, the unions cried, the case was bound to be lost, "but someday

Scene at Haywood trial, 1907. No. 1, Clarence Darrow.
No. 2, William D. Haywood.

Courtesy Idaho Historical Society

there would be an hour of reckoning." There was talk of calling a general strike all over the United States.

Late in July the trial approached the end. Darrow spoke for nearly eleven hours in his summation for the defense, holding the crowd in the courtroom and outside the door and windows by his emotional power. Although he had come to dislike Haywood intensely, he was magnificent with whatever cause he took up. James Hawley spoke for the prosecution, and William Borah concluded with a speech praised afterward for its fairness, even by Clarence Darrow and William Haywood.

Just before noon on Saturday, July 27, Judge Fremont Wood gave his instructions to the jury. A defendant was considered innocent, he impressed upon them, until proven guilty "beyond a reasonable doubt." They must remember that the testimony of an accomplice was often questionable; he might simply be trying to save himself. His testimony must be backed by other evidence. And the evidence must link Haywood to the Steunenberg murder, not to some other crime.

The jury filed out and the waiting began. Night came on and the crowd drifted away home, until only a few people hung around the courthouse. Clarence Darrow was so keyed up he couldn't sleep, he paced the streets all night.

At seven o'clock on Sunday morning, the jury foreman knocked on the inside of their door, and the bailiff unlocked it. The court was hurriedly summoned and the prisoner was brought in. Haywood slumped down in his seat, awaiting the announcement of his conviction.

"We, the jury, find the defendant, William D. Haywood, not guilty."

It was a bombshell. Haywood jumped to his feet, astounded. Pandemonium broke loose among his lawyers. Clarence Darrow dropped into a chair and broke into tears.

Borah hadn't arrived at the courthouse yet, but the rest of the prosecution sat shocked and silent. Governor Gooding was dumfounded. Crowds began to stream along Main Street, reading the newspaper "extra," hardly able to believe their eyes.

The jurors said, when questioned, that most of them felt Haywood was guilty as charged, but the "proof beyond a reasonable doubt" that the judge said was required, just wasn't there. Judge Wood, himself, believed the man guilty, but that was personal opinion and had no place in administering the law.

The results of the "Not Guilty" verdict were curious and unexpected. Both conservatives and liberals supposed it would strengthen the cause and methods of the violent element in the unions. The

Judge Fremont Wood and jury at Haywood trial, 1907.

Courtesy Idaho Historical Society

opposite proved true. The radical press had continuously declared that Haywood could not get a fair trial under our capitalistic system. Nevertheless, he had won acquittal. It seemed to be proved that a workman could get justice in a legal action even opposing the establishment. It seemed that justice could be obtained simply by the application of laws. A wavering faith in our system gradually found its way back.

The loss of leadership during the long absence of Haywood and Moyer contributed to the growing instability of both the Western Federation of Miners and the I.W.W. The miners were capable of violence, but they were not really much interested in economic and social theories. What they wanted was to improve wages and working conditions. They didn't care much about remodeling society or even improving relations between employers and workers. Sobered by their experience, the Western Federation freed themselves from their connection with the Industrial Workers of the World, and in 1911, rejoined the American Federation of Labor.

Although William Haywood seemed to have enjoyed the one peaceful year of his life, when he was awaiting trial (he planted a garden at the penitentiary, did a lot of reading, and even collected rose petals and made a little cushion to send to his invalid wife), the moment he was free, he again took up his violent life. In 1918, he was arrested with 94 other members of his union for sabotaging war efforts. Convicted in Judge Kenesaw Mountain Landis' court in Chicago, he was fined $10,000 and sentenced to twenty years in

Senator William E. Borah, age 42, at the time of the Haywood trial, 1907.

prison. While out on bail, he disguised himself and escaped to Russia, where he spent the remaining ten years of his life.

For some reason the Russians chose not to trust the American with any very important work, keeping him busy at obscure jobs. An army man, Colonel George Stewart, who had been an Idaho farm boy at the time of the trial, writes in his autobiography, "Years later I saw Bill Haywood once on the Red Square, walking with Trotsky, looking very dejected." However, when Haywood died, the Russians buried him in the Kremlin with their own heroes.

Harry Orchard, who pleaded guilty, was sentenced to hang, but the sentence was commuted to life imprisonment without pardon. Converted by the Seventh Day Adventist Church, he lived 49 years as a model prisoner at the Idaho Penitentiary. He operated a little shoe shop in the prison, and for many years tended the prison's turkey flocks, herding the birds in the hills back of the prison. In 1952, in collaboration with LeRoy Froom, he wrote his autobiography. It was titled "The Man God Made Again," referring to a verse in Jeremiah about a clay pot marred in the hands of the potter, who then formed it into a new vessel. He died in 1956, at the age of 88.

The title of his book appears as his epitaph on the bronze plate on his grave in Morris Hill cemetery in Boise: "Harry Orchard— The Man God Made Again."

Timberlands at Lake Coeur d'Alene.
(Syringa, Idaho's state flower, in foreground.)

Courtesy Idaho Dept. of Tourism and Industrial Development

Chapter 26

TIMBER-R-R!

WHEN OUR country was young, big lumber companies developed first in the New England states, and then around the Great Lakes. By 1900, the white pine forests of Michigan, Minnesota and Wisconsin were thinning out, and lumbermen turned their attention to the untouched forests of the Northwest.

Frederick Weyerhaeuser and John Humbird, timber owners and sawmill operators, sent a veteran timberman, C. O. Brown, to North Idaho to buy the best white pine lands he could locate.

Seven miles northeast of the present lumbering town of Headquarters, a trapper, for twenty dollars, guided Mr. Brown to the top of a towering rock (now known as "Brown's Rock"), and showed him the world's largest white pine forest.

For a timberman it was the thrill of a lifetime. Mr. Brown threw out his arms in a sweeping gesture. "We will select all the good timber that can be seen from this rock."

Tracts of this land had been granted to railroad companies in return for building railroads into the new country. From the railroads a company could buy "scrip," a certificate giving it the right to select a certain number of acres.

Very little of this Northwest land had been government-surveyed yet. A company that wanted to buy land had to survey it, itself, in order to get a legal description of the areas to file with the Land Office.

Mr. Brown found that the survey marker nearest to the land he wanted, was a township corner the Land Office had surveyed near the town of Pierce. A rival lumber company had already started surveying a line north from this corner toward the Beaver Creek drainage area, where the most valuable block of timber was located. Mr. Brown hadn't an hour to lose.

He had with him a crew of seven men. Through the heavy timber, five of them cut trail as hard as they could go for six days, while the cook and the seventh man hustled to keep the camp moving along with them.

When they reached the edge of the valuable block, two men started cruising timber (estimating by sections the kind and age of trees, and how best to handle their cutting), and the others began surveying a line back through the trail they had cleared to the township corner, making use of the line the rival company had already run.

Then off to Lewiston Mr. Brown rushed to file the list of descriptions they had worked out to cover the 30,000 acres, with the Land Office. Next day the rival company's man arrived to file, and ground his teeth in fury to find he was one day late. "We secured the land," Mr. Brown noted in his diary, "by the skin of our teeth." But big business is never satisfied with one win. Mr. Brown had railroad scrip entitling the Weyerhaeuser Company to select 20,000 more acres.

The fall rains had started and it was wet, cold, muddy and miserable. Nevertheless, triumphant with their first success, the crew threw themselves into the new race.

One day, after a week or so, Mr. Brown, checking through the timber, met a worker from a company they knew to be a rival for the land, and stopped to visit a few minutes. Either the man didn't realize who Mr. Brown was, or he was just careless, for he mentioned that his boss had just left for Lewiston to file claim to the land.

Mr. Brown rode lickety-split back to camp. By good luck the crew happened to be all gathered there. They excitedly debated what to do.

Brown's son, Nat, volunteered to ride to Orofino, sixty miles away, and telegraph the land descriptions to the Weyerhaeuser man in Lewiston, who could file for them as soon as the Land Office opened next morning. If their rival on horseback traveled by the regular train from Orofino, he couldn't arrive in Lewiston until 11 a.m.

Nat Brown had been cruising timber for two days in the rain, and had spent the night before in the woods without shelter, but he was young and tough. While the others hurried to fix up a rough list of the lands to be filed on, he ate a bite, saddled the best horse in camp, packed a lunch and a gallon of oats, and made a lantern of a candle stuck in a lard pail he could hang on his arm. At 3 o'clock he started out on the rough trail in the drizzling rain.

When it was almost dark, he got down to give his horse a feed of oats and light the candle. By the light, he noticed on the trail, recent horse tracks, traveling fast. Nat suddenly decided it was no time to take a break so he rode on, as fast as his horse could go.

Several hours later, when his horse was nearly spent, they came to a house and barn, called "Hatch's Stopping Place," and smelled the tantalizing aroma of hot coffee. Blowing out his candle,

Nat went up to the house and peeked through the window. A traveler was sitting at the table eating.

Although he was perishing for the comfort of a cup of that coffee, Nat turned aside and led his horse to the barn. Relighting his candle, he found two horses there. One was worn out and slathered with mud, one was fresh and saddled and ready to go.

Nat did not hesitate. Putting his own saddle on the fresh horse, he turned the other two loose, and started on.

He arrived at Orofino just before daylight and rode into the livery stable. A doctor was just riding in from a night call, and asked Nat if he was the man who had an engine waiting to take him to Lewiston. Nat, playing it by ear, said he was on his way to Lewiston. The livery stable owner, who also owned the hotel, said he was a little surprised, he had expected an older man, but gave Nat a letter of instructions to the engine crew, who were asleep at the depot, ordering them to take the bearer to Lewiston immediately. You can imagine what joy this unexpected gift of time brought to the wet and miserable Nat.

The engine arrived in Lewiston at 7 a.m. Nat woke the Weyerhaeuser representative at the hotel and they went to work straightening out their list of land descriptions. Then they headed for the Land Office and took their places in the line.

They had scarcely completed their filing when their competitor arrived, screaming for Nat's blood. Nat faded quickly from the scene while the man went after the sheriff. Nat went to a friend's house, where he slept the clock around while the friend hustled off to pay the railroad for the use of the engine, and arranged to have the borrowed horse returned. The Weyerhaeuser man checked hurriedly out of the hotel and crossed the river into Washington, out of Idaho's jurisdiction.

Taking the case to court wouldn't have changed anything, and in the end the rival company let it go. The Weyerhaeuser group had now accumulated 50,000 acres of the best white pine timber anywhere. This forms the main block of the white pine holdings of the present Potlatch Forests, Inc. For a long time the traditional policy of the lumber companies, "Cut out and get out," was followed in this area, but in 1929, they adopted a policy of selective cutting and reforestation. In 1943, they started their first tree farm.

If it seems to you that the ethics of the getting-there-first maneuvers recounted above were a bit tricky, you are probably right. The business test of right or wrong in those early days was the amount of money involved, and what you could get away with.

Grove of Ponderosa "yellow pine".

Courtesy Idaho Dept. of Tourism and Industrial Development

Success excused ways and means. You can decide whether we are different now.

If you drive along U.S. 10, the old Mullan Road, between Wallace, Idaho and Missoula, Montana you will see the old burn of the "Great Fire" of 1910, the most disastrous fire known in North America.

The fire started on the night of August 20, and lasted only two days, but so fierce it was, and of such velocity, it burned an area 160 miles long and fifty miles wide. Three million acres of timber went up in flame and smoke, four towns vanished, and an unknown number of people were killed, certainly more than one hundred.

Word first came from a telephone operator in Wallace, calling Mullan, who shouted that Wallace and the surrounding mountains were in flames and he would have to run for his life. Then the phone went dead.

Fire in the Forest.

Courtesy Idaho Historical Society

It had been the worst drought in twenty years. Not a drop of rain fell from April through August. The whole summer was a terror of little fires ignited by dry lightning. By August the district forester had drafted 10,000 men to fight the fires-loggers, U.S. Army troops, finally hoboes and drunks off the streets. By August 19 they had put out 3,000 small fires. At any moment the fall rains should start and their troubles would be over.

But on August 20, there was a hot, dry chinook wind. Suddenly north Idaho and western Montana exploded with what seemed spontaneous combustion.

The swiftness of the flames was unbelievable. They flashed up mountainsides and jumped across rivers. The white-hot heat and exploding gases set off thunderbolts, and started whirlwinds that tore up giant trees and tossed them spinning in the air. Fire raced through the treetops 150 feet above the ground.

The forest service crews and the people of the area fought bravely in the face of flaming hell. Elk City was saved by its women. All the men and boys were gone, and the wives and daughters fought all night on the rooftops, putting out blazes as burning fagots dropped out of the sky.

Most people seem to have come through the holocaust if they had a leader and obeyed him. Forest Ranger Ed Pulaski and a group of forty fighters were trapped outside Wallace and retreated to an old mine tunnel at the War Eagle mine; but the fire was so intense, it sucked the air out of the tunnel, and heat and smoke and gases poured in. Some of the men were panic-stricken and wanted to try to run for it. Pulaski knew that would be fatal, and stopped them with a gun. He had them lie on their faces in a trickle of drain water in the tunnel, while he kept changing a wet blanket over the entrance as each one caught fire, throwing hatsful of water at the flames creeping in. He saved 35 of the 40 men, until he finally collapsed, himself, and was unconscious for hours.

Soon after midnight on August 22, the humidity began to rise and the wind shifted. Light rain and snow began to fall, and the fires were dampened.

The 3-million acre wasteland changed the environment. Erosion of soil occurred, leaving large sections of bare granite. Thick brush eventually replaced the trees, and lodgepole pine followed. Lodgepole pine hasn't much value as lumber, but is used to make fenceposts, railroad ties, poles and pulp. An epidemic of bark beetles followed the edge of the burn.

The loss of some of our finest timber was irreplaceable, yet some permanent good did result from the terrible fire.

The Bernard DeVoto Memorial Cedar Grove along Lewis and Clark U.S. Hwy. No. 12 in the Clearwater National Forest.

Courtesy Idaho Dept. of Tourism and Industrial Development

Of all the enthusiasms of our most enthusiastic president, Theodore Roosevelt, the most ambitious was conservation of our natural resources.

Between 1901 and 1909, Roosevelt had set aside 148-million acres of national forest reserves, and created the Forest Service to take care of them. Gifford Pinchot was its Chief Forester, as dedicated a conservationist as Roosevelt. The purpose of the Service, he stated, was to see that the best use of the land was made for all of our people, present and future, and not for the enrichment of a few people and companies. The Service was to work to prevent fire, to destroy deadly insects and disease, to supervise grazing and timber cutting, and to protect the water supply.

These federal restrictions were not relished by the western states, which were young and poor and wanted to make a fast buck out of their resources, and never mind future generations. They organized a strong anti-conservation group in Congress, led by Senator Weldon Heyburn of Idaho, and fought to destroy the Forest Service by voting the least possible money with which to work. President William Taft, who followed Roosevelt, was concentrating his energies on trust-busting, and did not oppose the anti-conservationists. In the congressional session before the "Great Fire," the appropriation for the Forest Service was cut to one-half the amount of the year before.

After the fire, voters who hadn't paid much attention to how matters were going, suddenly awoke and began loudly to denounce Congress and the western legislatures for a national catastrophe. Because of the hot, dry summer, there would have been some fires anyway, but they might have been held under control if the Forest Service had had funds to build roads and trails and telephone lines into remote parts of the timberlands, and to stockpile tools and equipment for emergencies. If the representatives who had been elected to safeguard the voters' interests were interested in holding their jobs, they had better mend their ways.

This is the tone of voice that elected representatives hear most clearly. Money became magically available for the Forest Service. Congress even appropriated money to allow the federal government, the states, and private landowners to work together to protect forests from fire. The western states established fire prevention codes, and appropriated money of their own to back them up.

We have fires every year in our forests, started by people's carelessness and by lightning, and sometimes we have bad ones. But there has never been another, and we hope there never will be, as devastating as the fire of 1910.

Chapter 27

THE DESERT SHALL REJOICE

THE ONE ADDITION that could make settlement possible in Idaho was irrigation. The narrow panhandle in the north is squeezed between Washington and Montana and shares their green climate, but the volcanic layers and sagebrush plains of southern Idaho caused early mapmakers to label it part of "The Great American Desert."

The wagon trains toiling their way across the Snake River Plain were headed for California and Oregon and Washington. Not one of them was tempted to stop in Idaho. It was only when gold was discovered that people became interested in the area. When gold petered out, some of them searched about for other ways to make a living here. Living in Idaho is based on agriculture and is only possible with irrigation. The volcanic soil is rich with minerals because our rainfall is scant and they have been able to accumulate for millions of years without being washed away. But it takes water to make things grow.

The Hudson's Bay Company agents, Thomas McKay and Francis Payette, watered a big vegetable garden at old Fort Boise (near where Parma now is) in 1834, and how those green vegetables cheered dusty emigrants on their weary way west!

The Reverend Henry Spalding and his Nez Perce Indians started irrigating their gardens from Lapwai Creek in 1837. That first little project survived the destruction of the mission and is still in operation today.

A Mormon settlement at Fort Lemhi irrigated crops for four years, until the Indians ran them out. Then, in our first permanent settlement, Franklin, Mormons in 1860, dug by hand, a 3½-mile ditch from Maple Creek, and this ditch is still in use.

The raising of vegetables to sell began near the mines. Tens of thousands of miners living on beans and soda-bread and "sow-belly" were avid for something green to eat. It is said they traded gold dust straight across, weight for weight, for onions and carrots and cabbage and greens, and if this is a bit exaggerated, it is certainly true they were willing to pay a very high price.

Men began to settle along streams and build water-wheels and plant gardens and hay and orchards. The Davis brothers, Frank and Tom, located their farm where Boise City was later platted, and set out orchards on the present location of Julia Davis Park. This was halfway between the mining camps at Silver City and Boise Basin, and the Davises could pack their produce in both directions. Within a few years families were living on nearly every stream in southern Idaho. The permanent settlement of Idaho had begun.

Over the years Congress passed four pieces of legislation to encourage the settlement of our dry lands.

The first was the Homestead Act of 1862. A homesteader explained how it worked: "The Government bets you 160 acres against a five dollar filing fee that you can't live on the land five years without starving to death."

The second was the Desert Land Act of 1877, which gave a settler title to land, together with a water right. Under this Act, one million acres was settled in Idaho.

The third was the Carey Act of 1894, which brought the State into the irrigation business. The Act turned million-acre areas of Federal lands over to the State to arrange for settlement and irrigation. The Twin Falls tracts on both sides of the Snake River were developed under this Act.

The fourth and last piece of legislation was the Reclamation Act of 1902, which brought the Federal Government into the irrigation business, and still operates. Congress appropriates money

Sagebrush desert in Snake River Valley. "Three Buttes" were an emigrant train landmark.

Courtesy Idaho Dept. of Tourism and Industrial Development

to build dams and reservoirs and canals, and settlers pay back the cost to the U.S. Treasury within forty years, without interest. The Boise and the Minidoka projects were the first projects in Idaho to be developed under this Act.

Idaho is one of the lucky states because it has most of the length of the thousand-mile Snake River, fed by deep snows in the Rocky Mountains. But never, anywhere, is there enough water for the land that needs it.

Since water is so valuable and so scarce, you might expect it to start squabbles. You would be right. The words "irrigation" and "litigation" are considered very nearly synonymous in Idaho. Some lawyers specialize in irrigation law and spend their entire lives arguing water cases.

When there is trouble, the chief water-district employees to get into the action are the ditchrider and the watermaster. The ditchrider deals directly with the farmer, turning the proper amount of water into his ditch. In the early years the ditchrider rode horseback along the canal banks, with a holster on his saddle to carry a shovel. Later he took to a motorcycle, but the ditchbank was so rough he often ended in the ditch. Finally he bounced along in a beat-up Ford. The watermaster, who had an office but spent a lot of time trouble-shooting around the country, was the referee.

The source of irrigation.
Courtesy of U.S. Bureau of Reclamation

Water rights are very complicated. You don't buy irrigation water, you know, you only pay for the right to use it. The State grants you a permit. If you stop using the water, you lose the right to it. The permit is not for the use of a certain quantity of water, it is for the number of acres you have to irrigate.

The earliest water rights have a greater claim than later ones. In a year of plentiful water, that doesn't make much difference; but in a year when there isn't enough water to go around, it is cut off from late-comers according to the age of their water right.

The main thing to remember and the first rule an Idahoan should teach his children is, never monkey with another man's headgate.

There was the water war in the Teton Basin in 1935. The farmers around Rexburg, in the lower valley, had the oldest water rights; but the newer settlers, near Driggs, were in the upper valley and had first chance at the canal. Water was very scarce that summer, and the farmers in the upper valley began taking it all. The old settlers in the lower valley declared war and set themselves to keep the gates open so the water would flow down to them. The watermaster would go around the upper valley and screw down the headgates. The farmers would follow close behind and open them up. When they became too busy farming to be able to take care of it this way, they ran off the watermaster.

An extra man was hired to go out and measure the water in the Teton River and divide it up through the ditches. He was going to have trouble, so the water-district watermaster sent along a bodyguard. When the two men arrived at the main headgate, six white figures rose up out of the nearby brush, hooded and sheeted and rifle barrels sticking out under the sheets.   "Get out of here, strangers," said the leader, "and don't come back." The ditchrider and the bodyguard returned to talk it over with the watermaster. The watermaster telephoned the State Engineer and then the Governor and asked for troops. The next day the Buhl and Twin Falls companies of the National Guard arrived, and eight to a dozen men were assigned to each main headgate. After a few days things simmered down; the army went home, and the age of a man's water right, again, decided water distribution.

Two years before that, there was the dynamiting of the Mackay dam on the Big Lost River. The amount of water the Big Lost would produce was always uncertain, and 1933, was an especially low-water year. The situation was aggravated, because a construction company had acquired an area around Arco from the State under the Carey Act, built new canals to the Mackay dam and brought in new settlers. These new farms and canals were downstream from

The canal.

Courtesy U.S. Bureau of Reclamation

Farmer setting siphon tubes from main ditch into field.

Courtesy U.S. Bureau of Reclamation

Irrigating beet fields.

Courtesy University of Idaho Extension Service

Sprinkling potato fields.

Courtesy University of Idaho Extension Service

settlers with earlier rights, and the old settlers were up in arms. The case came into court and ended up with the judge operating the irrigation system for the season. Right off, in June, the watermaster displeased everybody with the way he divided the water. The old settlers got together and decided to take direct action. On June 21, they went into Mackay and bought some boxes of 60% dynamite at the hardware store, and went out to the dam. Two of them went to the gatekeeper's house to rip out the telephone and keep him busy, while the rest lowered a sack of dynamite into the lake, in front of the gate tower, and set it off. It blew a large hole in the tower wall and damaged the gates and trashracks, so that twice as much water poured through. Then they went on to the canals leading to the new farms and wrecked the headgates. Then they went home to supper.

As soon as the watermaster got the word, he brought men out and they tipped a raft up against the face of the gate tower to cover the dynamited hole. They got wool sacks from a sheepman, filled them with straw and weighted them with rocks, and lowered 330 of them against the crippled gates. In 24 hours, the water flow was back to normal. For the rest of the summer, changes in flow were regulated by removing or adding wool sacks.

"Never monkey with your neighbor's headgate."

A mass meeting was held soon after the dynamiting to consider the situation, and the Governor, a true Idaho man, sided with the old settlers. The construction company gave up and sold its rights in the downstream project at a marked-down sale. The law of earliest rights reigned again.

But don't think for a minute that the rule of headgates holds simply on big projects and large farms. Our neighborhood in Boise had water rights and we irrigated our lawns by flooding once a week. We splashed around with our shovels, a great pleasure on a hot day. Our turns were scheduled and one day, one rather impatient gentleman decided his next-door neighbor was taking too long, and without a word he closed her headgate and opened his own. His neighbor was an educated woman of social standing, a good Presbyterian, a gentle wife and mother. But when the water suddenly stopped running in her ditch, she went over to his yard with fire in her eye. And when the gentleman snapped back at her, without a moment's hesitation she lifted up her shovel and bashed him over the head.

Never monkey with your neighbor's headgate.

There was always some land with good soil, lying too high for the canals to reach. Optimistic settlers went ahead and tried to dry-farm it. There is no sight sadder than an abandoned shanty rotting in the hot sun in the middle of lonely acres once cleared and toiled over, now gone back to sagebrush and tumbleweeds and jackrabbits. When I was a little girl, there were hundreds and hundreds of these heartbreak houses in southern Idaho, and they gave me a scary feeling.

Today there is a happy sequel. Under the Snake River plains, ground water stores itself in a natural reservoir of tremendous size. It is fed by rain and snow, and by drainage of surplus water from normally irrigated lands. Also into this underground reservoir, the waters of the Big Lost and Little Lost Rivers sink through the lava fields near Arco. In the 1940s, men began to experiment with digging deep wells to reach this water and pump it into ditches on the high, dry lands, or distribute it through sprinklers. Have you ever seen anything prettier than sprinklers spraying water over green fields in a summer morning's sunshine? The experiment proved so successful, several thousands of these deep wells are now in operation. Good lands that were abandoned in the early part of the century have been reclaimed and produce fine crops, and have built fine homes and farm buildings. A danger is recognized that this steady drawing up of the underground water supply will in time reduce its amount, but our resourceful farmers will no doubt meet that problem when it comes.

Still another type of irrigation is being developed along high walls of the Snake River. Men are organizing to finance the pumping of the river water to heights over 500 feet, to raise it to the wonderfully rich plateaus that were ancient lake beds. Here are produced the finest potatoes and onions in the world.

For Idahoans, the most beautiful verse in the Bible is Isaiah 35-1:

"The wilderness and the dry land shall be glad; and the desert shall rejoice and blossom."

Sheep on the Sawtooth range near Stanley.

Courtesy Idaho Dept. of Tourism and Industrial Development

Chapter 28

SHEEP'S IN THE MEADOW COW'S IN THE CORN

STOCK RAISING IS by far Idaho's largest industry.

Cattle started arriving in the 1860s to feed the mining camps. Longhorns were driven up from Texas, herds came from Nebraska and California. For awhile Idaho was said to be one huge cattle ranch.

The men who brought them didn't plan to farm. They turned the cattle onto the free grass on the high ranges in summer, and brought them down to the free grass on the bottomlands for winter. They thought they really had it made. But there turned out to be some bitter, cold winters they hadn't counted on. In 1886, the Shoesole outfit lost two-thirds of a herd of 25,000 in blizzards in the Salmon River country. Two years later, the year of the "Big Freeze," a herd on the Little Lost River was nearly wiped out by a blizzard so fierce, it left the cattle standing where they froze. There were other things they hadn't counted on, too—drought, rustlers, and the Panic of 1893. Pretty soon the get-rich-quick operators began to fade out of Idaho.

Many small ranchers stuck it out and began to make a life of ranching. They got rid of early "cows is cows" breeds and got better stock. They raised hay and piled high stacks to feed their cattle when the thermometer went down. They built the beginning of permanent cattle raising in Idaho.

Sheepmen from Scotland started our sheep business, and Basques from the Pyrenees proved to be among the world's best herders. Sheep business became very popular for a time. Sheep are easier to handle than cattle, and they produce wool as well as meat. Prices went higher and higher. For a few years sheep were truly Idaho's glamour investment, and everybody who had some spare dollars put them in the sheep business—not just sheep ranchers, but doctors and lawyers and bankers.

Those rosy days faded away as the bottom dropped out of the price for lambs, and free range became more restricted. The doctors and lawyers and bankers went back to investing in gold mines in Mexico and oil wells in Canada. The sheep ranchers raised sheep on a smaller scale, or sometimes changed to cattle, which were, at that time, more profitable.

From the first there had been trouble over the free range. Isn't it curious that a man should feel so outraged that something he didn't have to pay for, had to be shared with other men? Every stockman felt he should have it all, himself.

Here in Idaho we never had such terrible range wars as they had in Montana and Wyoming, but we raised all the cain we could. Cattlemen shoved each other around the range. They warned sheepmen to get out and stay out, and when, of course, they didn't, there were sheepshed bombings and sheep shootings and poisonings. These activities were naturally not advertised very widely, they took place quietly after dark, and rarely was anyone caught.

Somebody did bring "Diamond-field Jack" Davis to trial. He worked for one of the big cattle outfits, and was accused of murdering two sheepherders. William Borah helped prosecute him and he was sentenced to hang, but the hanging kept being postponed, and after a few months a newly elected governor freed him. Mr. Davis took off for new lands, but the battle for free grass went on.

The poor stockmen were really put upon. They were busy enough fighting each other, and suddenly they had to find time to chase off homesteaders who had started fencing little ranches for themselves, under the Homestead Act of 1862. Cattlemen and sheepmen actually stopped taking potshots at one another long enough to put their wire clippers in their pockets and go out night-riding together.

In 1905, President Theodore Roosevelt decided the free grass out West must be getting pretty thin with all those sheep and cattle working at it, and he appointed a Land Commission to make some rules. The Commission mapped out Grazing Districts (this was the forerunner of our Bureau of Land Management), and further annoyed the stockmen by insisting they get grazing permits every year, at about half-a-cent an acre. It was pretty hard to enforce, at best. For example, the Boise Grazing District covered six million acres, spreading from Riggins to where Jackpot, Nevada now is.

In 1934, after the "Dust Bowl" brought our careless lack of conservation to public attention, Congress did some more legislating, passing the Taylor Grazing Act. Each grazing district was now to have an advisory board of twelve stockmen and one man to protect wildlife. It was hoped this would be an improvement, because "you might fool a Washington bureaucrat who didn't know which end of a cow stood up first, but you couldn't fool your neighbor on the next ranch."

Somehow this still didn't solve all the problems. Cattlemen and sheepmen on a board together were very much like India and Pakistan sitting at the same peace table. Then too, small ranchers claimed

The fall roundup.

Photo by Bob Lorimer
Courtesy Idaho Dept. of Tourism and Industrial Development

the big stockmen ran the boards to suit themselves, and the solitary federal man noticed that if the stockmen didn't approve of the way he operated the district, he was soon transferred somewhere else.

A new act took effect January 1, 1975, which will be interesting to watch. Nowadays other people besides stockmen have an interest in our public lands, and for the first time, the cattle and sheep interests are going to be offered some assistance in governing them. From now on, the districts are to have "fair-balance" advisory boards. Representatives of forestry, minerals, grazing, recreation, environment, watershed, lands, and county and state governments, are all to have a voice. The greatest users of a district will have the loudest voice.

What do you think, will this keep the peace?

Map of Wake Island.

Chapter 29

WAKE ISLAND PRISONERS OF WAR

MANY AMERICANS knew, long before Pearl Harbor, that when she was ready, Japan intended to wage war on the United States.

For years, when her merchant ships put in at Honolulu or our west coast ports, the crews (who were also reservists in the Imperial Japanese Navy) scattered with their tourist cameras and their notebooks to take hundreds of pictures, and to fill books with notes. Her ships circled our Pacific islands, noting information. Japanese fishermen came pathetically ashore at our islands seeking shelter and food; and while they were being sheltered and fed, they, too, noted information, on winds, tides and reefs, and charts of every rock and channel.

But there were many Americans who had set their hearts on peace at any price. When our Navy tried to interest Congress in air patrol bases on our Pacific islands, a storm of protest went up. We would offend Japan with our warlike actions, many claimed.

In 1932, Japan took over Manchuria and started southward, taking over China. The League of Nations protested. Japan walked out of the League of Nations. For nine years the large nations held conferences and protested. The United States protested about Japan's military activities 380 times. Sometimes Japan sent polite notes of reply; more often she didn't reply at all. And for nine years her military forces armed themselves and planned their strategy.

The United States finally became alarmed to the point of taking action. In 1939, Congress told the Navy to start building aviation bases on our Pacific islands and keep an eye on what was going on out there.

Wake Island was our nearest island to Japan. It was the last base to be started. In January, 1941, a construction force arrived and went to work. The company was a combine of top contractors called CPNAB (Contractors Pacific Naval Air Bases.) Because Morrison-Knudsen was one of the combine, 250 of the 1,200 men came from the Boise Valley.

They were mostly young fellows, some just out of college, some even younger. The pay was good and they wouldn't be gone long—they signed contracts for nine months to a year. It would be entertaining, a start at seeing the world.

Pacific islands are the tops of drowned, ancient mountain ranges. Wake Island is the very tip of an old volcano, its lavas enameled over with snow-white coral. It was a bird refuge, with millions of sea birds that were going to be a problem, both to airplanes and people. Wake was a rat refuge, too, thousands of hump-backed rats whose ancestors had jumped ship here, sometime back in history. There were hermit crabs, small scavengers wearing hand-me-down shells of other creatures that clicked unpleasantly as they went about their scavenging. There were sharks in the ocean, and stinging eels. The island was in the typhoon zone, too. A really violent typhoon had been known to wash the island clean; no point on Wake stood higher than 25 feet above the sea.

All this sounds uncomfortable, but Wake was a beautiful little island. It was shaped like a skinny wishbone, with a wonderful blue lagoon where Pan American Airways set down its Clipper ships to be refueled. The island was completely covered with brush and scrubby trees with big shiny leaves, and all over the ground grew moonflower vines that opened their white blossoms at night. And what a moon!

"We had a lot of fun," says a man who was there. "We went spear-fishing, and beachcombed for cowrie shells and Japanese fish-net floats to take home when we went. We swam in the lagoon where the sharks didn't come, and played baseball and tennis, and we put out a daily newspaper, the "Wake Wig Wag."

The contractor went all out to keep its workers content in this isolated spot. It had the best chefs that money could hire, and the meals were fine. There was a recreation hall, a library, and outdoor movies. True, no liquor was allowed, and naturally the boys tried to improve this situation by fermenting prunes and sugar into a drink they called "swipes," but it tasted so bad that it didn't cause much of a problem.

The civilian workers' superintendent was Dan Teters, the best kind of construction man. He was a big, pleasant Irish-American, a bear for work, but able to stay on good terms with his men. Under his handling, the crews accomplished an enormous amount of construction in a short time.

Important personages sometimes stopped briefly on the island while planes refueled. In mid-November, a Japanese diplomat, Saburu Kurusu, met the American officers for an exchange of politenesses on his way to Washington, D. C. to see, as he said, what he could do to improve relations between the two countries. Perhaps he was sincere, perhaps his government didn't tell him everything, either. At any rate it developed later that at the time he handed Secretary of State Cordell Hull a list of Japanese proposals on November 20, the Japanese fleet was already rendezvousing for its attack on Pearl Harbor.

Captain Scott Cunningham arrived at Wake November 28, 1941, as naval commander in charge of the island. He brought a small detachment of naval men, including a medical staff, and there were a few radio specialists.

Major James Devereux headed the defense battalion of 400 marines which was expected to be able to withstand a hit-and-run attack if it should ever come. To pass spare hours, 150 of the construction civilians volunteered for military training.

There was no radar. The equipment was on the dock at Honolulu, but for some reason it was never shipped. There was no warning system, either. They might not have been able to hear one, anyway, because of the pounding of the surf all day and all night. A lookout man, with field glasses, was posted on top of the 52-foot water tower. Telephone lines ran everywhere, but as it turned out, it was very unfortunate that they had not been laid underground. Under bombing attack they were among the first things to be knocked out.

On December 4, 1941, their long-awaited patrol planes arrived. Marine Major Paul Putnam and his squadron of 58 brought twelve stubby Grumman Wildcats. It developed that the bombs already stored on the island wouldn't fit the bombracks on these planes, but the do-it-yourself Americans contrived to hook the bombs under the planes with straps taken off practice bombs. Anyway, they thought, they probably wouldn't have occasion to do any bombing.

There had been no holiday for several weeks. Now, all forces decided to declare a holiday Saturday afternoon through Sunday. Men spread all over the island, fishing, boating, swimming, playing tennis and baseball. Sunday morning they slept late and took it easy all day.

It was a good thing they did. At 7 a.m. on December 8 (Wake is across the dateline—in Hawaii and the United States it was December 7), the radio man was stunned by the message, "Pearl Harbor under attack. This is no drill. This is no drill."

Four patrol planes took to the sky at once. No bunkers had been finished yet to protect the planes on the ground. The remaining eight Wildcats were spaced as far apart as possible on the parking area at the end of the runway. Captain Cunningham says the positioning was the worst decision of his life.

Less than five hours after Pearl Harbor was attacked, 36 Japanese bombers arrived at Wake under a cloud cover. The man on the tower didn't see them. Four patrol planes were flying at 12,000 feet, above the clouds, and *they* didn't see them. With the surf pounding, nobody heard them.

The three V-formations headed down the runway, bombing and strafing the planes and the men working around them. They flew over the contractor's camp and opened up with machine guns on men gathering for lunch. They wiped out the Pan Am buildings. They hit a 25,000-gallon aviation gas tank. Fuel drums exploded like firecrackers.

In twelve minutes, mission accomplished, the Japanese left for home.

The destruction was stupefying. The runway was one great crater, seven planes were destroyed, the eighth badly damaged. Three pilots lay dead on the parking lot, a fourth was seriously wounded. As the four patrol planes in the air returned to land, one was smashed in the wreckage on the airstrip and put out of commission, at least temporarily.

The island came up out of shock. There was no time to bury the dead. The bodies were carried to a large refrigerator-room in the contractor's camp. The wounded were taken to the hospital, also in the contractor's camp, and doctors worked over them through the rest of the day and all that night.

Wake is a skimpy island, less than 4 square miles in area, but it is practically all beach, with 21 miles of shoreline to defend. At each of the three points of the wishbone, Peacock Point, Kuku Point, and Toki Point, was emplaced a battery of heavy guns that had been taken off old World War I battleships. These were all right for level coastal defense, but were of no use against airplanes. There were some anti-aircraft guns that could be used against low-flying planes, but they were of no use against high-altitude raids. And there were enough anti-aircraft machine guns to space about one to every quarter-mile of beach.

Dan Teters volunteered to provide civilian work crews wherever they were needed, and to feed every worker on the island wherever he was working.

Bulldozers pushed up ground around the airstrip to make it too rough for enemy landings. Broken telephone lines were repaired. Camouflaged food dumps were located all over the island. Mechanics began working on two damaged planes, "cannibalizing" parts from the hopelessly wrecked ones. Guns were passed out to civilians, and ammunition supplies were cached and covered with coral sand. Foxholes were dug around the gun batteries, and in the protection of brush cover.

In exactly 24 hours the Japanese were back. This time there was no overcast and they flew in at 10,000 feet. The man on the water tower spotted them and shouted into the telephone. Twenty-five Japanese bombers left the contractor's camp in flames, including the hospital, barracks, machine shops and storehouses. The island patrol did shoot down one bomber.

Again everybody went to work. They took the ammunition out of two underground magazines and converted them into hospitals, where they carried the newly wounded and the patients who hadn't been killed in the bombing of the hospital. A third magazine was turned into a communications headquarters. Headlights of all vehicles were painted blue for night work.

The officers were convinced the Japanese had spotted Battery E guns, at Peacock Point. Working all night, 100 civilians jacked them up (each anti-aircraft gun weighed several tons), got them onto trailers, and moved them back one third of a mile. Where the battery had stood, they substituted dummy guns of wood and covered them with brush.

It was worth the night's work. When the Japanese came next day, they headed straight for the former Battery E position and gave the dummy guns a working over, while the real guns let go at them from the new location. About the only damage that day was the blowing up of a large supply of dynamite. One of the island's patrol planes shot down two of their bombers. The Wake Islanders felt better.

But in the night, 3 o'clock in the morning, ships were sighted on the horizon. There were six powerful searchlights located along the beaches, but Captain Cunningham kept them dark. The island remained perfectly quiet as the ships advanced. By five o'clock they were about four miles off.

There was a BOOM! from out there. Still, the island was kept dark and silent. The ships came zigzagging slowly closer. The island held its breath. At 6:15 the Japanese were beginning to put troops into small landing boats. A destroyer and some transports were in the sights of the heavy batteries. Captain Cunningham gave the order to fire.

The Island's success was great beyond anything they could have hoped. The ships had been enticed so far in that the gun crews had plenty of time to get ready for them. One ship blew up before their eyes. Others were hit again and again. The soldiers scrambled back onto their landing boats. Strangely, the Japanese had brought no planes to cover their landing. In forty-five minutes the ships turned tail and fled, with Wake's four Wildcats hot after them, loaded with the bombs that didn't fit the bombracks; their first chance to use them. They blew up a destroyer and set gasoline fires raging on decks.

This did help make up for that first raid when the Japanese inflicted so much damage and got away scot-free.

But the bombers began their daily raids again, while the island patched itself together every night. The Japanese knew exactly what they were bombing. Not once did they hit the water tower or the sea-water purifying plant they themselves would need later.

Word came at last that help was on the way. Ground troops, equipment and supplies were sailing from Hawaii. Another fighter squadron would come. This action may seem very dilatory to us, but the Pacific Command at this time was extremely busy in all directions. On the same day the Japanese bombed Pearl Harbor and Wake, they also bombed the Philippines, Hong Kong, Guam and Midway. But for the present, spirits on Wake soared. Civilians were to be evacuated.

Suddenly Japanese tactics changed. Twenty-nine dive bombers and 18 fighters arrived together, obviously from an aircraft carrier somewhere nearby. They concentrated on the island's guns. They came twice a day, in increasing numbers. The island was down to two patrol planes. One day one of those did not come back. The other was nursed back, all shot to pieces, and its pilot was carried to the hospital. Wake's air squadron was wiped out. What was left of its crews reported to the marine command for duty as infantrymen.

In the night of December 22, barges and landing boats were sighted near the shore. Captain Cunningham desperately radioed Hawaii for immediate help from any ships nearby. The answer came back; there were no American ships in the area, the relief expedition had been withdrawn within 24 hours of Wake Island, when Hawaii received information of the battle raging there.

This time there was no moon. This time the Japanese did not give away their location by firing their guns. They crept in silently through the dark until they were ready to invade. Then they swarmed ashore in the dark dawn of December 23. The men on Wake Island fought valiantly, but they were doomed by overwhelming numbers. In the end, a white sheet waved on a pole.

The American captives were kept on the island nearly three weeks before they were loaded on the ship, the Nitta Maru. On deck they had to run a gauntlet between a double line of Japanese sailors who kicked, slapped and struck them as they ran through, and also ripped off eyeglasses to stamp on them.

(The Japanese left more than 350 civilians on the island for work

Lt. Matsuda, Japanese military pressman from Shanghai, reads dispatches of English-American defeats and Japanese victories to civilian and marine prisoners-of-war at Woosung camp.
Copy of photo from Japanese propaganda magazine "Freedom"
Courtesy John Rogge

brigades. Later, all but 98 were taken away to Japanese prison camps. When it seemed likely, in 1943, that American forces were about to retake the island, on October 7, the guards lined up the 98 civilians remaining and machine-gunned them. In 1946, the War Crimes Commission heard evidence of this senseless atrocity, and sentenced several of the Japanese officers responsible, to be executed. The bodies of the 98 American victims were taken up and reburied at the National Cemetery of the Pacific in Honolulu.)

Of their nearly four years of miserable imprisonment, the twelve-day voyage on the Nitta Maru caused the prisoners the most suffering. They were sailing into winter weather in tropical clothes. Their only warmth came from being packed like cattle in the suffocating cargo spaces. They slept with two thin blankets on the bare steel plates of the ship. They were fed small amounts of thin, dirty rice soup. They were knocked about roughly on the least excuse.

One day five prisoners, three sailors and two marine sergeants, were brought on deck. No other Americans were present, but a Japanese crewman gave evidence to the War Crimes Commission after the war. He testified that Lieutenant Toshio Saito, commander of the guards, stood on a barrel and read, in Japanese, an indictment of the United States for killing Japanese. He stated they would now kill these five prisoners "for revenge." He gave the signals and the swords fell. The bodies were thrown into the sea. The War Crimes Commission sentenced four of the men who had wielded the swords, to hard labor for life, but Lieutenant Saito successfully disappeared from sight and was never caught.

Some of the prisoners were impounded in Japan, but most were taken to the Woosung Prison Camp near Shanghai, China. In mid-January the barracks were unheated, blankets were scarce and thin, and the Americans were dressed in their tropical clothing.

A starvation diet for prisoners was a matter of policy with the Japanese military; it kept energies low, and made men easier to handle. Everybody suffered from malnutrition. With some, tuberculosis and pneumonia followed. Dysentery and the diseases of malnutrition, pellagra and beri-beri were common. There were naval doctors among the prisoners, but they had no medical supplies.

However, the prisoners had one piece of good fortune. A Japanese army doctor who visited the prison camp regularly, was a man of humanity to friend and foe alike. Captain Yoshihiro Shindo is remembered with gratitude for easing their lives, and indeed, saving some of them, at considerable risk to himself, under the suspicious eyes of the Japanese military. Long afterward the former prisoners had the happy opportunity of doing something for him in return. The "Survivors of Wake" organization at a convention in Boise in 1961, heard indirectly that Dr. Shindo was living in Tokyo in want. They responded instantly with a collection to send him, along with warm expressions of their memories of his kindness.

The camp had its own prisoner cooks, but what could a cook do with small amounts of dirty rice that for some reason had little feathers in it, and tiny pebbles that broke their teeth? There was no salt available, and have you eaten rice without salt? There was tea that tasted as if made out of willow leaves, but at least it was hot.

The prisoners naturally became obsessed with thoughts of food. A friend of mine, whose brother died in the camp, has his diary. She says it is made up almost entirely of recipes.

"Oh yes," says the man who was there, "we thought about food all right. There was a guy named Hector who had been head chef at the Broadmoor Hotel in Colorado Springs. After we went to bed, we'd say, 'Come on, Hector, think us up a good meal,' and Hector would stir his memory and come up with all kinds of recipes for a fancy banquet."

Once, a work detail of prisoners returning to camp, found some chunks of rock salt in a box car that had transported horses. They brushed off the manure, sneaked the pieces back to camp, boiled the rock salt down and crushed it fine enough to use to season their rice. What an improvement, what a triumph!

The American officers were eventually allowed to plant a garden, and the famished prisoners fell on the vegetables like locusts. While the garden lasted, the Japanese cut down the rice ration.

By the 1929 Geneva Convention, agreements were signed concerning the treatment of prisoners of war. By this agreement, all civilian prisoners should have been exchanged back to their own countries. This and other rules of the agreement were brought to the attention of the camp authorities by American officer prisoners. The Japanese military triumphantly pointed out that Japan had not signed the Geneva agreements. She could make her own rules.

(The impossible problems brought about by this situation were the reason the Navy soon afterward organized the Seabees as its construction arm. It was obvious that civilians could not be allowed to work in war-endangered areas. Seabees are engineers and construction men, but they are also militarily trained.)

It was months before anyone in the United States knew what had happened to the men on Wake Island—whether they were alive or dead. In April 1942, rumor of the existence of Woosung prison camp filtered through to the Red Cross, and the names of some of the prisoners began to reach the United States.

In December, 1942, after nearly a year, the Red Cross was permitted to send in its first food package. In the remaining 32 months of imprisonment, the men received seven more shipments of food packages, and some clothing and blankets. Nothing more wonderful had ever happened in the lives of the prisoners.

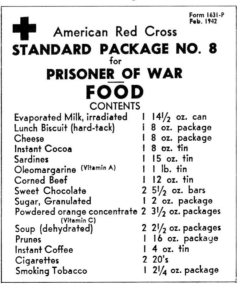

Prisoner of war Red Cross food package.

Courtesy John Rogge

"But I would like to make one suggestion," comments the man who was there. "Officers shouldn't be imprisoned in the same place as enlisted men and civilians. One Thanksgiving a wealthy bar owner in Shanghai named Jimmie James, sent us eighteen turkeys. There were 100 Allied officers in the camp, and they kept eight turkeys. There were 2000 of the rest of us, and we got ten."

The Japanese military were fond of long lists of detailed rules and regulations, promising death for the least disobedience. It naturally became a principle with the prisoners to get away with everything they could. They sometimes paid dearly for their principle.

The Japanese practiced a careless brutality on men in their charge, not only prisoners, but their own soldiers. Slapping a man across the face they didn't regard especially as a punishment, it was often done simply to emphasize an order-to indicate the man was to step lively. Since the Americans didn't understand Japanese, they received a lot of slaps. You can imagine the rage this would set off in an American. After a lot of trouble, the guards learned to say "Speedo!" in giving an order to an American. Anybody could understand that. If it didn't bring instant obedience, the guard beat him on the head with the butt of a gun. Anybody could understand that, too.

In the prison camps there were a lot of unpleasant things: rats, bed bugs, lice, and mosquitoes and flies in summer. But the most unpleasant thing at Woosung was a man named Isamu Ishihara, who for three years devoted himself to making life miserable for the prisoners. He was not an officer, he was an interpreter, but interpreters were scarce and he was valued by the authorities. In their game of nicknaming unpopular Japanese, the Americans called him "Beast of the East." He was tried by the War Crimes Commission after the war, and freely admitted the tortures he had dealt out, trying to obtain information on broken rules. He sincerely seemed to believe that any methods he used in the service of Japan could not be objectionable. In addition to this dedication to duty, however, the prisoners felt Ishihara really got some enjoyment out of smashing a man in the adam's apple with his riding crop, or beating him over the head with his samurai sword in its scabbard. The War Crimes Commission sentenced him to hard labor for life.

The general run of Japanese guards seemed to the prisoners rather like children. In fact some of them were boys in their mid-teens. They often lost their temper over some small thing, and yelled and waved their arms around, then in a few minutes would forget all about it.

The Woosung camp was a true melting pot. Besides the Amercans from Wake Island, there were marines who had been stationed in North China, and Chinese, Indians from India, Australians, New Zealanders, British, Italians, practically every nationality. Although Japan occupied this part of China, the International Settlement in Shanghai was still precariously in control of itself, and tried to get contributions through to make the prisoners' lives more comfortable. The risk was so great, there was very little they could accomplish.

The prisoners worked at many things. They dug ditches and canals, shoveled gravel, loaded coal, cut timbers for mines, built rifle ranges. The most hated chore was cleaning up shell cases to be used again for ammunition. The Americans became very clever at banging up the shells while polishing them, so they couldn't be used again. They got into a lot of trouble over this when the Japanese sergeant would look at a shell and shout, "No goodo!"

"We earned a little money," says the man who was there. "I was a coolie, I got 27 yuan a month. ('Yuan' was a unit of money the Japanese used in occupied countries.) 27 yuan wouldn't buy a ten-pack of cigarettes. I had one of the few pair of dice in camp. On payday I'd say, 'Come on, fellas, who wants to shoot 'em, all or nothing?' And when my pocket was full, somebody would borrow the dice, and it would go on till the camp was cleaned out, and a few of us would have money for a day or two. There was a lot of forbidden wheeling and dealing with the guards. There was a Chinese, not a prisoner, who came to work every day. We discovered we could slip money to him and ask him to get something for us from Shanghai. It might be two or three weeks before he could manage to get it. Sometimes he wasn't able to get it, and then he'd return the money to us. He wouldn't have had to, you know, we couldn't admit we'd given it to him. I got the idea the Chinese are mostly pretty honest. Do you think I'd go downtown in Boise and hand money to somebody I'd only seen three or four times, and expect ever to see it again? You bet I wouldn't."

Not everybody's hand was against them in this foreign land. The man who was there says, "The Japanese people are different from us, they're more hospitable and courteous. If I was an old grandmother living up in the Boise hills, and some dirty, ragged foreign prisoners marched past on their way from work, would I invite them in and give them tea? No, I would not! But an old Japanese grandmother did, for us."

"Another nice Japanese lady lived near the iron mine where we worked. She let us make a fire near her place, and sometimes she gave us a little food, though she didn't have much for herself. We made it up to her when we got a Red Cross package. We rode up to the mine on narrow ore cars, and when we went ka-klunk ka-klunking past her place, we'd throw packages off for her."

In spite of starvation rations, illness and low energy, the Americans managed to achieve some creative triumphs. Boys with electrical knowledge hooked into wires to heat water. Later, out of metal scraps, they built an electric hot-plate. Some with carpenter ability, built a dentist chair and other dental equipment, and barbershop chairs. Individual prisoners weren't allowed razors, but a few elderly barbers were permitted to use some very ancient straight razors. They sharpened them on a brick.

The Americans were passionately interested in finding out how the war was going. The Japanese authorities were happy to inform them of Japan's triumphs and American defeats, but the prisoners hoped there might be some news less discouraging. Men with radio experience finally concocted a short-wave radio. To keep it from being confiscated, each part was carried by a different prisoner. Two or three times a week the parts would be assembled, and one man would get under his blanket and put on the headphones, and relay the war news to the others. This succeeded for nearly two years. For a long time it wasn't much of a comfort, the news was so bad, but it gave the prisoners the feeling of connection with their own people.

Even in the fine arts, something was achieved. Prisoners who could draw, sketched prison camp life on every scrap of paper they could get their hands on. The sketches were rolled up and hidden in empty Red Cross shaving cream tubes. Here the artists immortalized the prison camp authorities they hated, and got rid of some dangerous steam in doing it.

The Americans were very busy with one thing and another, but their supreme occupation was finding something to laugh about, and one of the favorite ways was to think up nicknames for hated guards and officers. "The Screaming Skull," "Useless Yusi," "Horseface," "The Ape," "Handlebars," "Mortimer Snerd." Mortimer was a little suspicious about his nickname, but the prisoners explained that Mortimer Snerd was one of America's most popular movie stars. The guard was pleased, and the prisoners were overjoyed.

"There were all kinds of funny things," relates the man who was there. "There was a great tall British prisoner named Willie, who had been made the goat-keeper. Every morning the guards would come by, shouting 'All out! All out!' and we'd line up to be counted. Then here would come Willie to open the gate to the goat pen, and shout 'All out! All out!' And we'd die laughing."

It was considered great sport to frustrate the guards by refusing to suffer under punishment. "The Red Cross sent us some little stoves. It was great because it was winter and very cold. There were very strict rules about the stoves because the Japanese are scared silly of fire. When somebody didn't put a fire clear out, his whole unit would be punished. They all had to march around with somebody carrying the stove and a big sign, 'I did a bad thing, I didn't put the fire out,' or some such, and we were all supposed to feel very punished. But we thought it was the most comical thing we'd ever heard of, and we'd go goose-stepping around, laughing fit to kill."

"And once somebody stole some rice and nobody would admit it. The guards turned everybody out, stark naked in the middle of a winter night, snow on the ground and the leaky water tower one huge icicle, and made us run around in a circle while the guards beat us across the backs with sticks. Suddenly one boy was inspired to hold his hands as if around handlebars, and go putt-putting and sputtering and backfiring like a motorcycle. And in half a minute every single prisoner was putt-putting and sputtering and backfiring and laughing like fools. It just drove the guards crazy."

American boys are wonderful. Don't ever forget it.

Several escape attempts were made. Sometimes a group got away successfully, but they were always captured within a few days.

The first attempt was made by Naval Captain Cunningham, Dan Teters who had been civilian superintendent on Wake Island, two Britishers and a Chinese. For two weeks they planned carefully, choosing a dark night. Dan Teters was in charge of the tea department in the kitchen galley, and he was able to get the long-handled shovel he used to shovel tea out of the vats, so they could dig a trench under the electric fence and crawl under. They made it without being electrocuted, and hid in a barn, but next day they were caught. They had expected that any Chinese farmer would help them reach the Chinese guerrilla army, but the risk to any Chinese was too great. He turned them in to the Japanese.

The most serious situations sometimes produce something ridiculous. The escape of prisoners reflected on Colonel Yusi, the camp commandant, and he was terribly humiliated. He rounded up some mongrel dogs which he thought would act as bloodhounds. He took them to the fence where the men had dug their trench, and let them smell some clothing belonging to the escaped prisoners. Then he turned them loose to show him which way the prisoners had gone. The dogs took one sniff of the air, and headed for the kitchen!

Not admitting that prisoners could escape from them, the Japanese had no rules for dealing with such a situation, so they court-martialed them as "deserters from the Japanese army!

The recaptured men were sentenced to varying years of imprisonment in the Shanghai Municipal Gaol. In this jail, men were even more closely confined than in prison camp, and they rubbed on each other's nerves more, too. Captain Cunningham in his "Wake Island Command," writes of a lot of bickering and rowing around. Then a funny thing happened. Among books contributed to the jail inmates by the Shanghai Red Cross, there chanced to be a copy of Dale Carnegie's "How to Win Friends and Influence People." The book went the rounds of the prisoners, and for a short time, Captain Cunningham says, they really made an effort to control their tempers. Wouldn't Mr. Carnegie be pleased!

In the early summer of 1945, when the war was running strongly against Japan, she began to move her prisoners of war to camps in Japan. As the trains passed through the country, the blinds were pulled down tight to prevent the prisoners seeing the bombing destruction of the countryside. Peeking through the slats, the Americans began to feel more cheerful.

In the Odati prison camp, work went on for the prisoners much the same, in iron mines, carpenter shops, steel mills. In one of the steel mills they were fortunate in having as director a kindly and courageous Japanese, Mr. Gando. When they were ill, as they often were in their run-down state, he would hide them, at the risk of his own life, so that the guards would not make them work. Warm friendships grew out of this humanity and survived the war, leading to reunions years later.

The bombing was becoming continuous. The Americans' first sight of B-29's was a heartening thing, but it was nerve-wracking too. What if, after everything, they were to be bombed by their own countrymen!

After August 14, without explanation, the guards stopped sending out the work crews. The prisoners lay around waiting, rumors flying.

And then, on August 17, over the public address system, there came a message from the Emperor to his people. "The last All-Clear has sounded," it said. "Go into the streets and greet the Americans nicely."

Food drops and leaflets began falling from B-29s soon after. The prisoners learned about the atomic bomb, about Hiroshima and Nagasaki.

It took some time for arrangements to be made to fly the healthy prisoners home, and get the ill ones on board the hospital ships Haven and Sanctuary. While they were waiting, an incredible fact emerged. One of the boys brought out of his pocket a tiny American flag, hardly

"Made in Japan" 1945.   Courtesy T. Bailey Lee, Jr.
Photo by Bob Newell

two inches across, which he had managed to keep hidden for nearly four years. It simply wasn't possible, with the constant searches they had been subjected to—but *there* was the flag. Some of the men were suddenly inspired to make themselves a flag and fly it over the camp.

They didn't have anything to make a flag with, but that was a minor difficulty. Imagination was supplied by an Idaho man, T. Bailey Lee Jr., who in civilian life was a 170-pound Morrison-Knudsen excavation superintendent, but by now was a 95-pound prisoner who mended Japanese uniforms. When officers had asked for a volunteer tailor he had risen to the opportunity and declared he owned a tailor shop in the United States.

He cautiously borrowed some needles and khaki thread from the workroom, a ship's linen sheet, and a red silk Japanese quilt. Lee couldn't risk stealing scissors, so they cut the 48 star holes very precisely out of heavy blue Australian dungarees with a chisel. The men sewed it all together firmly with a baseball stitch, seven red silk stripes, six linen-colored stripes, forty-eight white stars showing out of a field of blue.

They worked all night to finish their three-by-five foot flag before sunup, and then they ran it up the staff to ripple over the Odati prison camp—certainly among the first American flags to fly in Japan after the war.

It was a beautiful flag. It is a beautiful flag today. Those boys knew just how it should be. In three years and eight months in prison camps under a foreign flag, they had learned all there is to know about their American flag.

Note: A thrilling tape, "The Story of Wake Island," produced by Dar Dodds, one of the returned prisoners, can be borrowed by schools from the Idaho State Library, 325 W. State St., Boise, Idaho 83702.

Chapter 30

OUR JAPANESE

JAPANESE WERE THE last nationality to come to the United States, because until 1884, Japan did not allow her people to migrate. After that, workers came to the Hawaiian sugar plantations by the hundreds, and in fewer numbers came to the California coast to work on railroads, farms and fishing boats.

They were not welcomed. As Orientals, they inherited the ill will given to Chinese during our gold rush. It is a curious and un-lovely fact of human nature that some of us seem to need somebody to hate, preferably somebody of another race we don't know very well. Some New Yorkers hate Jews, some southerners (and northern-ers too, for that matter) hate Blacks (and some Blacks hate Whites), some Texans hate Mexicans. In California, some people decided that Japanese-Americans should be their special hate.

In the beginning there were probably reasons. Workers and labor unions feared the effect of many immigrants on wages and employment. Also, in 1905, Japan defeated the Russian navy and began to grow proud of her strength, making dwellers around the Pacific Ocean uneasy about the future. Once started, hate doesn't need reasons; it feeds on itself. Organizations began to form for the single purpose of putting down our Japanese-Americans. Poli-ticians and newspapers, finding it a popular cause, began to sound off about it all across the country.

During World War I the noise died down somewhat, because Japan was an ally. As soon as the war was over, the hue and cry was raised again, even more loudly.

Japanese immigrants could not become citizens and could not own land. However, their American-born children, who were auto-matically citizens, had a citizen's right to own property, and some-times parents managed to buy land in their children's names. The land that people were willing to sell them was not very good land, usually marshy or desert or with alkaline soil. Since the Japanese were wonderfully skilled gardeners, and hard-working and patient, they were often successful even in bringing such poor land into pro-duction. Then, just as with the early Chinese miners, Caucasian neighbors sometimes began to covet these improved lands for them-selves, and added their voices to fanatical editorials and broadcasts warning that Japanese-Americans had a sinister plan to get possession of all our farmlands.

After such a chilly reception on the Pacific Coast, the Japanese didn't move inland in any great numbers. In 1920, there were 1569 Japanese in Idaho, going busily about their gardening and minding their own business. But their enemies on the Coast, seeking support, wrote to our chambers of commerce and our legislators. I can remember the alarm of my parents' generation over the "Yellow Peril" that was about to take over the United States. In 1921, a bill was introduced in the Idaho Legislature to petition Congress to withdraw citizenship from all people of Japanese descent.

At this point a troubled Boise Congregational minister called a mass meeting of citizens in January, 1921, to consider whether our Japanese were being treated "with truth and justice." Some ignorance and misinformation was cleared up, but fanatical voices across the country were louder and more persuasive. In 1924, Congress passed the Exclusion Act, which closed admission to any immigrants not eligible for naturalization. This act, barring all Orientals, was our law for 28 years. It was not lifted until 1952, seven years after World War II was ended.

When war broke out with Japan in 1941, our government set up military control of a strip about 100 miles wide along the coasts of Washington, Oregon, and California, and Arizona's border with Mexico. From this strip the Army ordered the removal of all people of Japanese ancestry, as a safeguard against possible treasonous acts. In the first panic after Pearl Harbor, there were wild accusations (later proved false) that some Japanese Hawaiians had secretly assisted Japan. Immediately, aliens were required to register, and federal agents searched their homes, taking away cameras, radios and guns.

Three terms much used during World War II to classify Japanese-Americans, were:

"Issei" (e-say)—first-generation immigrants.

"Nisei" (ne-say)—American-born children of Issei parents.

"Kibei" (ke-bay)—Nisei who had gone back to Japan for their schooling. The Kibei were regarded with particular distrust by our military as being probably sympathetic to Japan.

One hundred and ten thousand Japanese were moved from the coast military area to ten "relocation centers" scattered over territory farther inland. This did not satisfy the racists, who demanded that everybody of Japanese descent be locked up until the war was over, and then shipped to Japan. It is to the credit of most of our

*Airphoto section of Hunt Japanese-American Relocation
camp near Minidoka, 1942.*

Courtesy Idaho Historical Society

churches that they stood firmly against these rabid voices from
beginning to end.

One of the ten centers was the Hunt Relocation Center built
on federal land near Minidoka, Idaho. At its peak this instant town
had a population of more than nine thousand, making it the eighth
largest town in Idaho.

The location was not a very cheerful sight to the evacuees from the
green coasts of Washington and Oregon. It was desert sagebrush
land, absolutely bare, deep with dust, where the wind blew nearly
every day, hot in summer, cold in winter.

The camp was laid out according to standard military design.

Three and one-half miles long, one mile wide, it was made up of rows of tar-paper barracks in units of twelve, each unit called a block. With each block was included a messhall, a recreation hall, laundry and lavatory buildings, to serve 250 people. Each long barrack was divided into six rooms, 20 by 24 feet, with a family in each room. The government furnished each person with an army cot, pad and army blankets. Beyond that, the families were to build their own furniture out of scrap lumber. Some barracks were set aside for schools, classes to be taught through grades and high school, and another barrack served as a hospital.

When the evacuees began to arrive in August, 1942, the Hunt camp was nowhere near finished. The carpenters tried to keep ahead of the arrivals but never quite made it, and for the first few months many families had to double up, perhaps hanging a blanket for a partition in their one room. This got things off to an uncomfortable start.

The evacuees' nerves were already pretty frazzled. They had been given so short a time to sell or store their possessions and make ready to move, that unscrupulous people cheated them out of land and homes and businesses they had spent a lifetime building. They were worried about unsatisfactory arrangements they had been forced to make for possessions left at home and could not now change.

Their most immediate discontent came with the food served at the messhall. It could hardly have been worse. The War Relocation Authority committed itself to feeding these thousands for an average of 45 cents per person per day. For several weeks it averaged even less than that because of the difficulty of getting food shipments. If you think a meal costing about fifteen cents wouldn't be very satisfying (even in those days of lower prices), you are right. And good humor doesn't come from an unhappy stomach. Tempers were ready to flare.

The evacuees noticed one day that a contractor was building a barbed-wire fence around the camp, and were enraged. They were not supposed to be prisoners, they were temporary residents between homes. In the dark of the night some of them slipped out and cut wires and dug up fenceposts. This naturally infuriated the contractor next morning, and without asking anybody, he electrified the fence. The Japanese exploded like firecrackers. "Concentration camp!" they screamed, marching on the administration building. The authorities hastily set the contractor straight, got the fence disconnected, and publicly apologized to the evacuees. The situation simmered down but they remained sore and suspicious of the government's intentions.

It was not only the authority of the administration that irritated them, it was each other. There were as many different kinds of people among them as you would find in any normal town of that

Group of Japanese-Americans at Hunt Relocation camp near Minidoka, during World War II.
Courtesy Idaho Historical Society

size but here they were all crowded together. There were grand-parents and babies and all ages between. People who were brilliant in their professions, and laborers who couldn't read or write. Buddhists and Christians and atheists. Dispositions of every variety. And there were, as in any large group, a few people who enjoyed stirring up the coals of discord, and spreading unpleasant rumors.

The family unit too, had trouble holding its traditional pattern. Food and shelter were furnished by the government, so that a father was no longer the family provider and its authority. With the lack of any privacy in family life, and the mixed assembling for meals, it was difficult for parents to maintain the discipline of their children.

College students were worried about the interruption of their education. Churches over the country were the first to recognize this danger to morale, and made a big effort to get the students out of re-location centers and back into colleges.

The dislocation of their lives may have been hardest on the older men. They had lived all their lives in traditional Japanese ways and hard work, and now these things were taken away from them. They pottered about, raising little gardens. They played hours of "goh," Japanese checkers, and they gambled their few dollars at card games. If they could whittle, they carved flower plaques for the walls, and name markers for their doors. In the evenings they walked for hours in the desert or along the canal, looking for a stone shaped or colored in a particular way, to add to their doorstep garden. In years to come, all the buildings would be hauled off to serve some other purpose, and the towers and pipes and concrete would vanish, but here and there would still remain these arrangements of little stones and cactus that once marked entrance-ways as special to one particular family. Perhaps in a more personal way than any other race, the Japanese possess the talent of expressing beauty with simple things.

With so much that was worrisome, it is pleasant to find that not everybody put in three years fretting and stewing. A few years after the war I met a young Nisei in his oriental shop in Seattle. It developed that he had spent part of his boyhood in the Hunt relocation camp. Asked if he remembered it with resentment, he laughed. "We kids had a ball," he said. "We'd never had so many other kids to play with. We played baseball and basketball, and had a band, and saw movies, and practiced judo, and swam in the canal."

But the ones who really enjoyed themselves were the older women. They had generally led lives of drudgery. Now, with only one room to keep in order and no cooking to do, they took to leisure with immense pleasure. They took English classes and sewing and Japanese singing and handicrafts of all kinds. In a poem she wrote for her Japanese poetry class, one woman expressed herself:

> "Fortunate me! Indifferent
> To the fierce fighting
> All over the world,
> Here I am, learning
> Flower arrangement, writing, and embroidery."

In spite of a few flare-ups, the Minidoka camp was one of the most peaceful of the relocation centers. A lot of things improved. In the spring of 1943, the evacuees grubbed out sagebrush and cleared rocks and dug ditches, and planted 250 acres of vegetables. Being from the coast, they had had no experience with irrigation, but even with natural mistakes, they raised tons of vegetables. In the year following, they increased these cultivated acres to 800. A hog ranch and a poultry farm were started. As the meals improved, so did dispositions.

The evacuees operated a cooperative general store, repair shops, barber and beauty shops. There were a lot of camp jobs open to volunteers at set salaries of $12 to $19 a month. Leaves of absence could be obtained to work outside the center at regular wages. Because of the war shortage of workers, and because Japanese were almost invariably good workers, they were very welcome on the farms of Idaho, Oregon and Utah.

After Pearl Harbor our armed forces stopped induction of Nisei. Very soon, however, our intelligence service was in desperate need of men who could understand Japanese. Recruiters went to the relocation centers and screened 167 men to translate captured documents and interview prisoners. The Kibei, who had been educated in Japan and had been the most distrusted by our military, proved the most useful of all in this work. Some were also established in Portland to gather information from short-wave radio. These men working for our Intelligence, the military called our "secret weapon."

By 1943, our panic had worn off enough so that the military decided to form a special Nisei combat team and see how it would work. From the Minidoka camp 300 volunteers applied, and two-thirds were accepted. Their fellow-evacuees held flag dedication ceremonies for each group departing for training camp, and each messhall displayed stars for the number of volunteers from that block.

The 442nd Combat Regiment built a heroic legend in the European war. Nine thousand five hundred Nisei fought with it at some time during the war. About 1,200 came from the relocation centers, and a much greater number from Hawaii. The notable 100th Battalion of Nisei National Guardsmen from Hawaii ("the most decorated unit in U.S. military history," was the offical rating they earned) served as one unit in the 442nd. The motto of the 100th was "Remember Pearl Harbor." The motto of the entire 442nd Regiment was "Go For Broke."

It may be they were inspired by these mottoes, and by the blue emblem on their shoulders with its proud white Torch of Liberty. Or it may be they were fired by a determination to prove themselves the best American fighters who had ever fought. At any rate, in September, 1943, they went over from North Africa to the tip of the occupied Italian peninsula, and for eight months pushed their way slowly up through Italy, forcing the tough German armies out of their trenches in all those terrible, deadly battles that read like a geography lesson—Salerno, Cassino, Anzio, Rome, Belvedere, Bologna, Genoa.

American newspaper correspondents began to write back to their papers about the "star-spangled courage" of the Nisei. "They don't call themselves 'Nisei,' " one wrote. "They call themselves simply Hawaiian or American. And our doughboys in the cold mud and rocks and hills of this bleak Italian front will tell you, 'They've earned the right to call themselves anything they damn please.' "

When Italy was won, the Nisei fought in France. It was here, in rugged, forested mountains, that the 100th Battalion fought its most celebrated battle, the rescue of "The Lost Battalion" of Texans. Three hundred men of the 36th Texas Battalion were in a German trap, cut off from water and supplies, and set up to be butchered. The

100th Battalion of Nisei boys picked their way across 2½ miles of mines and booby-traps, with fearful losses. Snatched from annihilation, the Texas boys threw their arms around them and hugged them till they yelped. The rescue of these 300 men cost the Nisei 800 casualties.

On July 15, 1946, what was left of the 442nd Combat Regiment paraded down Constitution Avenue and was presented the Presidential Distinguished Unit Citation by President Truman.

With the success of the combat team, Nisei began again to be drafted under selective service in 1944, the same as any other Americans. They fought with Merrill's Marauders in the China-Burma-India area, and they fought in the Pacific.

America's most noted Nisei war hero was Ben Kuroki, small in stature, mighty in valor. Ben, "The Kid from Nebraska," enlisted in the Air Force the day after Pearl Harbor, before our military clamped down on the induction of Nisei. As a tail-gunner, he flew 29 missions over Europe. Then he requested service in the Pacific, and flew 29 more, finishing in a B-29 bomber named "The Honorable Sad-Saki." Then he was sent on a speaking tour through California to plead in Japanese-hating communities for tolerance toward returning evacuees. This must have taken more courage than all those missions in the tail of a bomber. He had considerable success, being a modest, unassuming chap telling it the way it was. He so impressed the Commonwealth Club of San Francisco, that at the conclusion of his talk, they gave him a ten-minute standing ovation.

You may be surprised to know that some of the anti-racists were still in there, sniping away. After so much bitter war, you would think all the hate in the world would be used up, but prejudice is the habit we hang onto longest. With the returning of evacuees to the coast area, there were some incidents of burning and dynamiting buildings, night-shooting into homes, signs in store windows, "No Jap trade wanted." The most spiteful, most low-down act was the chiseling off of sixteen Nisei names from the War Honor Roll of one community. That was finally going too far. Aroused citizens went into action to redeem their town from shame, and within two weeks the sixteen names reappeared on the Honor Roll.

A lot of people began to get into the act. Interior Secretary Harold Ickes in one of his vitriolic speeches, blistered the West Coast for acts of terrorism and local law enforcement bodies for not controlling them. Caucasian officers who had fought with the 442nd Regiment went into hostile neighborhoods and told their story. The War Relocation Authority, about to be disbanded, went up and down the Coast helping fair-minded citizens organize programs to fight prejudice. Gradually all this combined persistence won out over the shrill voices of narrow minds.

About two thirds of all evacuees returned to their homes on the Coast. Despite discouragement over vandalized buildings and stolen possessions and betrayal by neighbors they had counted as friends, the Japanese Americans took up their lives and started over. In 1952 the Exclusion Act was repealed and an immigration quota was assigned to Japan. Japanese immigrants can now be naturalized the same as any other nationality.

Not many evacuees at the Minidoka center returned to the Coast. They scattered all over the United States, turning their energies and abilities to every business and profession, as well as to their traditional magic with orchards and gardens.

It has been our good fortune that 3,500 evacuees chose to make their home in our state, taking their place among Idaho's most loyal, productive and successful citizens.

Atoms for Peace.

Courtesy Idaho Dept. of Highways

Chapter 31

ARCO'S ATOMS

I N THE SPRING of 1949, Life Magazine hailed Arco, Idaho, as the most excited town in the United States. Arco was on the point of having the Atomic Energy Commission select its backyard for a Nuclear Reactor Testing Station, to perform all kinds of amazing experiments with materials that can produce atomic energy.

The site required three things: an immense area of vacant land; a plentiful supply of pure water; and nearby communities willing to absorb extra thousands of workers.

Every community in southeastern Idaho was willing (how willing!) to house the workers. The Snake River Plain had all the vacant land anybody could wish for. And beneath the Plain, there was a vast underground reservoir of water. A deep well was drilled through the lava, and water was pumped up to be tested for purity.

Betty Marvel, the wife of Arco's mayor, was with the group at the well when the result was announced.

"You would have thought it was an Indian tribe out there," she says of the scientists taking part. "They whooped and they shouted and they danced around, and one of them said to me, "Mrs. Marvel, this is something to tell your grandchildren about!""

Construction started right away. The station, in all its multiplicity, covers 572,000 acres, and cost half-a-billion dollars. It has a working staff of about 5,000.

There is practically nothing in the atomic world that our testing station hasn't tested. Every atomic reactor built in the world today has been given assistance by the N.R.T.S. at Arco. Deputy Chief Emelyanov of Russia's Atomic Energy Commission, says "It is a college of nuclear research that all people who design and build reactors should attend."

In its few years, the station already has a record of important achievements. Probably the best known is the nuclear engine developed for the submarine, Nautilus. This engine illustrates the way we can turn the heat produced by smashed atoms, into energy we can use. It heats water to steam to operate a turbine to turn the propellers to move the submarine. Very like the house that Jack built. The advantage of the nuclear engine to a submarine is that it doesn't have to surface every now and then to recharge its batteries and load up with oxygen. Its atomic fuel will pay itself out for 30,000 miles which is a considerable voyage. After the Nautilus, the N.R.T.S. developed a nuclear engine for the carrier ship, Enterprise, and one for the missile cruiser, Long Beach.

But we are supposed to be finished with war. The primary purpose of the station is to develop uses for atomic energy in peacetime, and the greatest immediate need is to develop electric energy in a time of desperate shortage. A survey made for the Atomic Energy Commission indicates that, at our present rate of use, and increasing population, we will run out of coal and oil deposits before the year 2075. A pound of uranium will produce 2,600,000 times as much heat as a pound of coal. The trouble is that it takes such an enormous quantity of ore to produce a pound of uranium, and the deposits are scarce.

That is our problem with atomic power, the scarcity of fissionable (capable of producing energy when their atoms are split; "fission" means "a splitting apart") materials. The only known fissionable metals are uranium and plutonium, and plutonium is, itself, derived from uranium atoms.

Now there has been a breakthrough in a discovery that scientists can produce ("breed") a synthetic uranium from another mineral, thorium, which is less rare. The N.R.T.S. now operates what it calls a "breeder reactor" to produce this synthetic uranium. There is a deposit of thorium in Idaho, in the Lemhi Pass area, near Salmon, larger than all known uranium deposits in the United States.

An interesting experiment is being carried on in the Raft River area, where there is much underground hot water. Scientists are testing hot water wells for the possibility of using them to develop power.

And how about Arco, all this time after that exciting spring of 1949? Well, it didn't get much of a share of those 5,000 workers. Most of the workers went to Idaho Falls to live. Before "The Coming," Arco's population was 780. It hasn't doubled that figure yet.

But Arco had its moment. It may not be the largest city on the Snake River Plain, but on July 17, 1955, it became "the first town in the free world to be served by electrical energy developed from the atom." (Four light bulbs glowed for two hours.) Nobody can take that away from it.

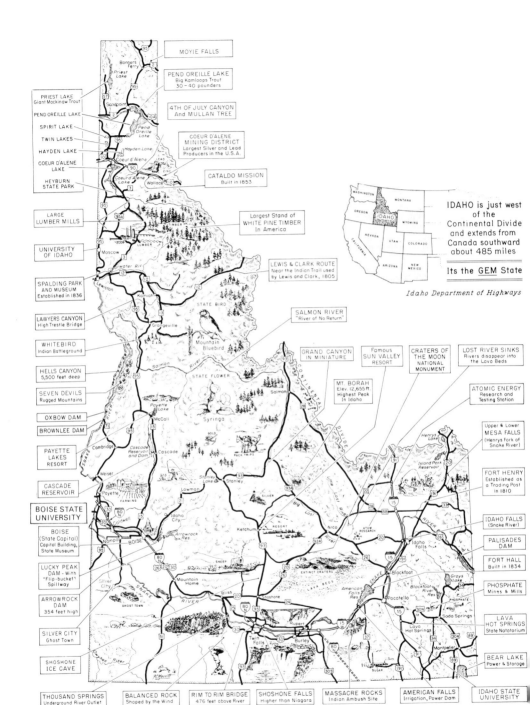

MOYIE FALLS

PEND OREILLE LAKE
Big Kamloops Trout
30 - 40 pounders

4TH OF JULY CANYON
And MULLAN TREE

PRIEST LAKE
Giant Mackinaw Trout

PEND OREILLE LAKE

SPIRIT LAKE

TWIN LAKES

HAYDEN LAKE

COEUR D'ALENE
LAKE

HEYBURN
STATE PARK

COEUR D'ALENE
MINING DISTRICT
Largest Silver and Lead
Producers in the U.S.A.

CATALDO MISSION
Built in 1853

LARGE
LUMBER MILLS

Largest Stand of
WHITE PINE TIMBER
In America

UNIVERSITY
OF IDAHO

SPALDING PARK
AND MUSEUM
Established in 1836

LEWIS & CLARK ROUTE
Near the Indian Trail used
by Lewis and Clark, 1805

LAWYERS CANYON
High Trestle Bridge

SALMON RIVER
"River of No Return"

WHITEBIRD
Indian Battleground

GRAND CANYON
IN MINIATURE

Famous
SUN VALLEY
RESORT

CRATERS OF
THE MOON
NATIONAL
MONUMENT

LOST RIVER SINKS
Rivers disappear into
the Lava Beds

HELLS CANYON
5,500 feet deep

MT. BORAH
Elev. 12,655 ft.
Highest Peak
In Idaho

ATOMIC ENERGY
Research and
Testing Station

SEVEN DEVILS
Rugged Mountains

OXBOW DAM

BROWNLEE DAM

Upper & Lower
MESA FALLS
(Henrys Fork of
Snake River)

PAYETTE
LAKES
RESORT

FORT HENRY
Established as
a Trading Post
in 1810

CASCADE
RESERVOIR

BOISE STATE
UNIVERSITY

IDAHO FALLS
(Snake River)

BOISE
(State Capital)
Capitol Building,
State Museum

PALISADES
DAM

LUCKY PEAK
DAM - With
"Flip-bucket"
Spillway

FORT HALL
Built in 1834

PHOSPHATE
Mines & Mills

ARROWROCK
DAM
354 feet high

LAVA
HOT SPRINGS
State Natatorium

SILVER CITY
Ghost Town

SHOSHONE
ICE CAVE

BEAR LAKE
Power & Storage

THOUSAND SPRINGS
Underground River Outlet

BALANCED ROCK
Shaped by the Wind

RIM TO RIM BRIDGE
476 feet above River

SHOSHONE FALLS
Higher than Niagara

MASSACRE ROCKS
Indian Ambush Site

AMERICAN FALLS
Irrigation, Power Dam

IDAHO STATE
UNIVERSITY

IDAHO is just west
of the
Continental Divide
and extends from
Canada southward
about 485 miles

Its the GEM State

Idaho Department of Highways

SOURCES
(Idaho's Place in the Sun)

Early History of Idaho .... *William J. McConnell*
History of Idaho .... *Merrill Beal and Merle Wells*
History of Idaho .... *Hiram T. French*
History of Idaho .... *John Hailey*
Idaho in the Pacific Northwest ... *Floyd Barber and Dan Martin*
Idaho of Yesterday .... *Thomas B. Donaldson*
Idaho—Student's Guide to
   Localized History .... *Merle W. Wells*
A Short History of Idaho .... *Idaho Historical Society*
Files of IDAHO PIONEER
Files of IDAHO STATESMAN
Files of IDAHO YESTERDAYS
Historical Articles by Dick d'Easum
Historical Articles by Arthur A. Hart
Adventures of Captain Bonneville. *Washington Irving*
All Along the River .... *Nellie Ireton Mills*
Americans from Japan .... *Bradford Smith*
Americans in Disguise .... *Daniel Okimoto*
The Appaloosa .... *Francis Haines*
Astoria .... *Washington Irving*
The Basques in Idaho .... *Pat Bieter*
Big Bill Haywood and the Radical
   Union Movement .... *Joseph R. Conlin*
Boise, the Peace Valley .... *Annie Laurie Bird*
Builders for Battle .... *David O. Woodbury*
Bury My Heart at Wounded Knee. *Dee Brown*
Captain Bonneville's County..... *Edith Haroldson Lovell*
Exile of a Race .... *Anne Relploeg Fisher*
The Far East—A Modern History. *Nathaniel Peffer*
Farewell to Manzanar .... *Jeanne Wakatsuki Houston*
The Fur Traders .... *Washington Irving*
The Good Years .... *Walter Lord*
Henry Harmon Spalding .... *Clifford Drury*
Historic Silver City .... *Mildretta Adams*
History and Origin of the Basque.. *Joe V. Eiguren*
History of Japanese-American Re-
   location Center-at Hunt-Minido-
   ka, Idaho (Thesis for Master of
   Science in History-Utah State
   University-1964) .... *Donald E. Hausler*
Idaho—American Guide Series ... *Works Progress Administration*
Idaho Almanac—Territorial Centennial Edition-1863-1963